Franchising on a Shoestring

Making franchising work for you . . .
without breaking the bank

Daphne Clifton

A & C Black • London

First published in Great Britain 2008

A & C Black Publishers Ltd
38 Soho Square, London W1D 3HB
www.acblack.com

A CIP record for this book is available from the British Library.

ISBN: 9-780-7136-7543-6

This book is produced using paper that is made from wood grown in managed, sustainable forests. It is natural, renewable and recyclable. The logging and manufacturing processes conform to the environmental regulations of the country of origin.

Design by Fiona Pike, Pike Design, Winchester
Typeset by RefineCatch Limited, Bungay, Suffolk
Printed in Spain by Graphycems

CONTENTS

ACKNOWLEDGEMENTS

In putting together this book I have drawn on my own business experiences, both the positive and the more challenging. Much time has also been spent researching the experiences of those committed to the world of franchising, either as franchisees or franchisors. My thanks go particularly to the following people and businesses who have given of their valuable time: my ever-patient son, James, who has fed and watered us both; John Byrne and Judy Lowry, my coaches who've kept me on track; a number of friends and colleagues who have offered their experiences of franchising as case histories. In particular, Stephanie Manuel of Stagecoach was most generous with her time; Lisa Carden at A & C Black for giving me the opportunity to stretch outside my comfort zone by writing this book and having every confidence in me; the British Franchise Association (BFA), which has kindly agreed that, when helpful, its information can be reprinted here; Roy Seaman at Franchise Development Services (FDS), who has taken time to offer a deeper level of understanding in the franchise business; Richard Holden and the franchise team at Lloyds TSB, who have kindly agreed that their material can be reprinted when appropriate; and Chris at Franchise Advice, who has offered and provided a wide range of information along the way.

INTRODUCTION

Before stepping any further into this book, be sure to understand that, despite the series title, you can't operate a franchise or set up a franchise on a shoestring. This book is part of the on a Shoestring series, but what we mean by the phrase in this case is making the best use of the resources you have available, and spending them wisely. Franchising is one option that can help you do that: it allows you to run your own business, as a franchisee, without having to re-invent the wheel. And as a franchisor, it gives you the opportunity to expand your network with a proven business model.

To illustrate what a diverse sector you are entering, the Natwest/British Franchise Association (BFA) survey 2008 tells us that there are around 809 franchisor systems within the UK with 32,400 franchisees and territories. The annual turnover is £12.4 billion[1] and 383,000 people are in franchise-related jobs. It's worth noting that women[2] are at last making their presence in franchising known. In the past 10 years, the

---

1 Source: BFA
2 Source: Which Franchise.com

number of UK franchisors looking specifically to recruit women has tripled. This has been reflected in the increasing numbers of successful women who are now running their own franchise businesses across a wide variety of industries – health and fitness, fast food, B2B, cleaning, estate agencies, home furnishing, pet care, children's services, gardening, beauty, printing, care services – to name just a few.

A franchise is an agreement enabling a third party to sell or provide products or services that are owned by a manufacturer or supplier. The franchise is granted by the manufacturer (the *franchisor*) to a *franchisee*, who then sells the product. Franchises operate in a wide variety of industries, from fast food chains to will writers and gardening experts, and there's a huge amount of choice. The danger is that in entering the market, you feel like a kid in a sweet shop with so much to choose from that you don't know where to begin. To make the decisions more manageable, each chapter of this book will consist of the following elements:

- Introduction
- Key points
- Things to watch out for
- Helpful resources

Rather than writing one book for franchisees and one for franchisors, this book looks at both perspectives so that you get a rounded picture of what each party wants (and needs) from the other for the franchise to work successfully. Some elements will, of course, be more relevant for franchisees than for franchisors and vice versa, and I have made it clear to whom I am speaking along the way.

No book can offer solutions for every challenge that comes its readers' way, but I hope that this one will help answer some common questions and give you the confidence to make a success of your venture. There are bound to be those amongst us who 'busk it', 'go with the flow', or 'trust their gut instincts' when it comes to making business choices. There's nothing wrong with that, when it works and you don't have dependants. If you run or operate a franchise, though, you'll be heading up a team who will be depending upon you to be successful. You will be investing hard-earned or borrowed cash into your business and you'll want to see a return on that investment! By all means trust your gut instincts, but do support them with hard facts. As Bill Gates says, 'Success is a lousy teacher. It seduces smart people into thinking they can't lose.'

1 THE LANGUAGE OF FRANCHISING

As part of your investigations into franchising, it's worth taking time to understand the language used as it can be complicated, unclear and, at worst, confusing. Throughout your investigations, be sure that you understand each step of the process. As a franchisee, you will be running your own business and must manage it closely at all times, being clear about what is happening at all stages. Part of that understanding comes through using the right language and not giving up until you are clear on what is expected of you and what you can expect of the franchisor (or vice versa if you are the franchisor). As a franchisor, you need to be completely clear in the language you use and what you are communicating.

Most business language is the same, with similar principles applied. Of course there will be terminology appropriate and helpful for the franchise business. Take time to look at the glossary of terms (below) and be sure to ask a decision-maker at every stage if you are unsure of what is being expressed.

When employing a lawyer or accountant, make sure they are familiar with the world of franchising. There is a comprehensive list of affiliated professional advisors on the British Franchise Association website. Be sure to talk to two or three before deciding who to work with. Culture will be important here: you must have a good rapport with your lawyer or accountant. And cash – what will be their fees?

Avoid ambiguity

As with any language, there can be ambiguities along the way. Whether you're communicating verbally or in writing, have the confidence to ask for clarification if there's even a remote possibility that you are or could be confused.

As you consider options, sign agreements and communicate with potential and existing business partners, listen out for vagueness or very general terms. For example:

- you **may** earn up to £1 million per annum
- you **could** receive 20 leads per week
- this is **likely** to be a profitable business

None of these are certainties. What does '**unbeatable** training' really mean? And '**continued** support' could be one phone call a month or weekly training for which you will be asked to pay additional costs. Phrases such as 'you **will**' and 'we **guarantee**' are more positive, but still be sure to check out exactly what they mean for your set of circumstances, and have all agreements backed up in writing.

Communicate simply and clearly

Popular though business jargon is (and if you've seen *The Apprentice*, you'll know what I mean), there is no need to fall into the trap of using it. There will be some terminology that you'll need to get to grips with (see below), but that doesn't mean that you can't ask questions or use simpler language to check that you've understood.

The alphabetical glossary below covers the key expressions you will see and read when living in the world of franchising.

Area development franchise – This type of franchise will include the rights to expand a region through appointed sub-franchises or multiple managed outlets. It may also be described as a regional franchise.

BFA (the British Franchise Association) – The organisation set up to regulate the industry on an ethical basis. The Association has a Code of Ethics and Procedures, and those franchisors meeting its criteria are granted membership. Check out its website at www.theBFA.org. The BFA highlights the following as the benefits of becoming a member:

- public recognition of having met the Association's established standard, and being among the best in franchising
- increased public awareness of member franchises through BFA PR, franchise guides and monthly e-magazines with a circulation of 20,000
- being part of the authoritative voice of franchising, lobbying UK and European governments in the interests of franchisors
- inclusion on the BFA website which provides members with more than 14,000 leads for prospective franchisees each year
- access to discounted schemes for exhibitions, advertising and other benefits
- eligibility for the BFA Franchisor and Franchisee of the Year awards
- national and regional forums, bringing the best advice and latest news in franchising
- the BFA franchisor mentoring scheme, providing access to the best network of franchise experience
- a regular news service, keeping members up to date with the BFA and broader franchise issues

- access to exclusive BFA training programmes
- access to cost-effective dispute resolution procedures
- assistance with the international development of member franchise networks
- participation in the BFA's national programme of franchise seminars

Block exemption – The European Union concessions to franchising. These bypass the normal EU anti-restrictive trade practices legislation which seeks to protect competition – for example 'exclusive areas' can be deemed to contravene it.

Brand – A collection of images and ideas representing an economic producer. More specifically, the word refers to the concrete symbols of the producer, such as a name, logo, slogan and design scheme. Brand recognition and other reactions are created by the consumer's accumulation of experiences with the specific product or service, both directly relating to its use and through the influence of advertising, design and media commentary. The brand – and 'branding' and brand equity – have become increasingly important components of culture and the economy, now being

THE LANGUAGE OF FRANCHISING

described by marketing professionals as 'cultural accessories and personal philosophies'.

Business format franchise – This is where you buy into a whole package, called a 'total turnkey system', which will include the brand, know-how, training, methodology and support.

Buyback – If a franchisee no longer wants to continue with his or her franchise, the franchisor may agree to buy it back. If you're a franchisee in this position, it's important to understand what you have delivered to the business, how you've grown it and the value that it offers. We're back to knowing your business inside-out, how it ticks and what it's worth.

Costs – There will be fees involved in the purchase or sale of a franchise, whether it be for solicitors, brokers or accountants. Both buyers and sellers need to find out who is responsible for which costs. Remember that you may well regret your economies if you take short cuts in the early stages of buying or selling a franchise.

Decision-maker – The person or people who are in a position to make a decision about something – that is, whoever is 'signing on the dotted line' in whatever deal you are doing, for example the person at the franchisor who can authorise your marketing spend.

Disclosure – The practice of revealing detailed information about the franchisor's business track record and franchise package. This is a legal obligation in the US but voluntary in the UK. Finding out this kind of information must form part of your due diligence. Check out the situation for the country relevant to you: visit the British Franchise Association's website for more help here.

Due diligence – The process you go through to establish the viability of the franchise you wish to buy or set up. This involves taking a detailed look at the promises being made to you, and gives you the opportunity to see how they stack up. There should be a prospectus available to you with information about the business so you can establish its worth. If this isn't available, you will need, at the very least, to ask for the last two years' accounts and customer, staff and equipment lists where appropriate. Leave no stone unturned with your due diligence (see Chapter 6 for more on this).

Exclusive area – This may also be called a 'territory' and is the area licensed out to franchisees in which they may conduct business. Check out 'exclusivity' carefully; this will, or should be, defined by the terms of the franchise contract (see below).

Fees – The amount of money and frequency of payment agreed between the franchisor and franchisee. This must be stated clearly in any agreement.

Franinfo – This is a complete source of franchising information, offering a comprehensive directory of UK and Irish franchises for sale, as well as expert franchise and business focused advice and news. Franinfo is also the official website (www.franinfo.co.uk) for the UK Franchise Exhibitions, which are exclusively supported by the BFA.

Franchise contract – This can also be known as the 'franchise agreement' and is a document that defines the legal relationship and obligations existing between franchisor and franchisee.

Franchise fee – There are two common types of fee: initial and ongoing. The initial fee is sometimes called the 'front-end fee'. It is a one-off payment designed to cover the franchisor's costs of recruiting and setting up the franchise. The ongoing service fee, or 'management fee' (see 'Management service fee', below), is most commonly based on a percentage of sales turnover. It is the usual way for the franchisor to obtain his or her continuing income from the franchisees. Occasionally a franchisor will choose to charge a fixed fee on a weekly or monthly basis. Beware of this (see Chapter 5, Continuing fees section).

Franchisee – The person who buys the licence to replicate the business system.

Franchise package – This is the total offering purchased by the franchisee, and includes all the licensed rights, branding, know-how, systems, territory, training and so on, for which an initial fee is charged by the franchisor.

Franchising – Simply put, this is a method of marketing goods and services via a business formula that is licensed for others to copy, usually in exchange for an initial fee, a percentage of gross sales or profits, and some annual fees (see Fees above).

Franchisor – The company or individual that offers the licence to replicate their business system.

Franchisor News – This is the only publication

exclusively for franchisors. The magazine provides the latest news, features and advice.

Intellectual property – The franchisor's secrets of doing business and various trademarks, copyright, methods of producing and/or processing, branding, manuals etc. which should be legally protected before being sold in a franchise package (see also 'Know-how', below). This is important in order to protect the business – imagine how you'd feel if you had a great business idea which someone else copied, protected in their name and then stopped you using!

International Franchise Association (IFA) – the franchise trade association for the US.

Job franchise – This is where the franchisee is a hands-on owner/operator rather than a manager (usually linked with van-based services, such as maintenance).

Joint venture franchise – Common in international franchise agreements, in a joint venture franchise the franchisor also takes a financial stake in the project. For example, some leading UK high street chemists will offer an optician's franchise in order to secure that part of the market. Joint venture franchises are both highly prized . . . and highly priced.

Know-how – The sum of the franchisor's secrets of doing business (see 'Intellectual property' above).

Licence – The operating package licensed to the franchisee by the franchisor.

Management service fees (MSF) – This is the correct term for what many refer to as 'royalties'. Paid by the franchisee to the franchisor, the MSF is often based upon total turnover and likely to be around 10% of gross (less VAT).

Management franchise – A franchise in which the owner manages the operation and coordinates employees to do the work.

Marketing – This is a tool you use to sell your product or service.

Marketing plan – The 'A Team' always has a plan; no-one ever dies and they always win! This is the plan of how you are going to implement your strategy – putting the flesh on the bones, if you like. You should do this plan at least once a year.

Marketing strategy – Big-picture insights that guide marketing activity, giving high-level direction to all that you do. Your strategy must give you an over-arching goal.

Master franchises – These are franchise opportunities that have a proven system in another country, but have not entered the UK as yet. The franchisee will be bringing in the system and must evaluate the benefits against the risks carefully.

Master franchisor – The master franchisor is the person or entity granting master franchises to others. This is usually in an international context.

Operations manual – The detailed document or 'bible' which describes every element of the business system and work procedures.

Patch – See 'Territory/area' below.

Pilot operation – An independent operation which tests both the franchise concept and the actual financial, organisational and logistical pressures to be faced by franchisees in different areas.

Profit and loss (P&L) projections – These are the calculations based on the experiences of the franchisor, pilot and existing franchisees, which try to predict how soon new franchisees can expect a return on their investment, year-to-year turnover and profits. P&L projections are a really important element of your franchise investigations, so engage a reliable accountant to help you with this and to ensure you are living in the real world when it comes to your investment in any franchise business. See also 'Return on investment' below.

Prospectus – A printed document describing the chief features of the franchise opportunity.

Pyramid selling – A marketing system, erroneously associated with franchising in the past, which involves selling distributorships through a tiered structure. The founders of such schemes rely primarily on selling distributorships rather than products. Several Acts of Parliament govern pyramid selling in the UK.

Regional franchise – See 'Area development franchise' above.

Renewal – This refers to the legal provisions in the franchise agreement for renewing or not renewing the franchise for a further term of years. Be clear about this from the outset: you don't want to lose a profitable business or discover you require further capital investment to continue the franchise.

Re-sale – This refers to a franchised area that is already established by a franchisee. It is offered for sale because the original franchisee wants to realise his investment, move on or simply retire. This is more

THE LANGUAGE OF FRANCHISING

expensive than buying a 'virgin' franchise area, but comes with the advantage of an ongoing customer base, referrals, goodwill and income from day one of operating.

Return on investment – The calculations or expectations which franchisees work on to assess when they can break even on their initial investment in the franchise and start earning profits. See also 'Profit and loss (P&L) projections' above.

Roll-out – The process of taking one outlet and replicating it in a number of new areas, for example nationwide if it's a national roll-out. Think of rolling out the red carpet.

Royalties – Traditionally, royalties are paid on copyrighted works of art such as literature and music, where different tax arrangements apply. This is not the correct expression to use in the world of franchising (see 'Management service fees' above). In fact, if the term is used within a franchise, it may raise questions with the Inland Revenue.

Sale agreement – the document listing all elements of the franchise business involved in its purchase by the franchisee. The sales agreement will give you some comeback should things go wrong (for example, faulty equipment or misleading information such as inaccurate accounts). Do *not* try to save money by buying a business without a proper written sale agreement.

Soft loans – These are basically business loans where little or no personal collateral is required as security for the loan.

Sub-franchisee – This is a subordinate level of franchisee to a regional franchisee or area developer, usually appointed after the regional or area franchise has set up a training and support infrastructure for the territory. Be sure to understand all the relationships here. (This is not covered specifically in this book.)

System – The franchise model being used to run the business.

Target audience – The primary group of people that something, usually an advertising campaign, is intended to appeal to. A target audience can be people of a certain age group, gender, marital status etc. – for example, teenagers, females or single people. A certain combination of these factors – men aged between 20 and 30, for instance – is often a target audience. Other groups, although not the main focus, may also be interested. Discovering the appropriate target market(s) to aim a product or service at is one of the most important stages in market research. Without knowing the target audience, a company's advertising and selling efforts can become difficult and expensive.

Term – This is the number of years for which a franchise is granted through the franchise agreement.

Termination – Specifically this refers to the conditions under which either party in the relationship may legally terminate the contract (breach of contract, for example). The sun may be shining on your venture at the start, but make sure the agreement contains proper provisions in the event that things don't work out, so you know how to 'close' with the minimum of damage to all parties.

Territory/area – The 'exclusive' portion of land on a national, regional, county or postcode basis which is allocated for trading to franchisees as part of the franchise package. It also be referred to as a 'patch'. Activate your cynicism and questioning techniques when learning how areas are allocated.

Trading Act – This is better known as the Trading Schemes Act (1965), which was introduced to combat the excesses of 'pyramid selling' in the 1980s. It is valuable in that it distinguishes franchising from such dubious schemes. Today, the diluted offspring of pyramid selling are often to be found in magazines covering 'network marketing' or 'direct selling', where it is still the norm to earn money chiefly from recruiting subordinate levels. For more information, visit the Department of Business, Enterprise and Regulatory Reform online at www.berr.gov.uk.

Turnkey – A commonly used term describing a situation where the franchisee turns the key in the door with the business ready to run.

WIIFM factor – The 'what's in it for me' factor, which speaks for itself. Customers, franchisors and franchisees will all have this in mind during negotiations of any type. Everyone wants a good deal and, if running a business, will have an eye for their profit.

Key points

- Use common language for common understanding. It may be stating the obvious, but if you're new to franchising you must remember that this is your business and that you must be sure you understand what's going on around you at all times.
- Ask for clarification to improve your understanding.

■ At various stages of your investigations into franchising, you must be clear about what you need and why you need it.

Things to watch out for

■ Jargon can easily confuse matters. Those who've been in the franchise business for a while may want to impress, or may have merely forgotten that certain words are franchising jargon.

■ Familiarise yourself with new terminology, looking for specific examples that help to clarify your understanding.

Helpful resources

British Franchise Association (BFA) – **www.thebfa.org**

www.whichfranchise.com – the official online partner of the BFA

Franchise Advice – **www.franchiseadvice.co.uk**

Franchise Development Services (FDS) – **www.fdsfranchise.com**

Franchise Magazine – published bi-monthly, the publication often has a jargon-busting section

Your lawyer or accountant – ask him or her for clarification of legal/financial language

The Plain English Society – **www.plainenglishsociety.net**

WILL FRANCHISING WORK FOR YOU?

'EVERY MINUTE YOU SPEND IN PLANNING SAVES 10 MINUTES IN EXECUTION. THIS GIVES YOU A 1,000% RETURN ON ENERGY . . . !'

Brian Tracy[1]

Now is your opportunity to take a look at whether buying into or setting up a franchise will work for you. Simply put, franchising is a method of marketing goods and services via a business formula that is licensed for others to replicate, usually in exchange for an initial fee, a percentage of gross sales or profits and the annual fee (sometimes referred to as the 'management service fee'). Some of the biggest businesses in the world are franchises — McDonald's and The Body Shop among them — but they are a vibrant source of growth among small businesses too.

1 *Eat That Frog*, Hodder Mobius, 2004

If you're reading this book, you're either in a position where you have an existing business that is ready to expand, in which case you will become a franchisor, or you are in a position where you want to run a business using an already tried and tested formula, in which case you will become a franchisee. If you fall somewhere in the middle and you have an idea that you think can 'go global', refer to Chapters four and six. You'll need to go away, make your business model work and then come back to franchise it.

As a franchisee buying in to a franchise, you will be running your own business with a kick-start from an established brand. You will be responsible for each element of running that business, including:

- sales and marketing
- cash collection and accounts/investment
- managing a team
- customer satisfaction
- meeting your franchise agreement responsibilities
- administration
- planning for the future
- anything else required to keep the business running successfully!

As a franchisor, you will be responsible for all the above with your existing business, plus:

- developing and protecting your brand
- investing in franchisees
- marketing and training materials
- recruiting, training and motivating franchisees
- long-term research, development and innovation
- anything else required to keep your franchise ahead of the game!

These areas of responsibility show that if you decide to go down the franchising route, you'll need to take your decision carefully and seriously. Managed well, picking up an existing business model to work with is a great idea that can bring out the entrepreneur in you. The flipside can be that your creativity may be limited by the franchise agreement. If you feel strongly about this, it may be that franchising isn't for you.

If you think you can sign up to a franchise, sit back and let it happen around you, you are much mistaken. There are some important questions to address with your short-, medium- and long-term goals in mind, and you need to think about them at the following levels:

1 personal
2 family
3 business

Below are some simple questions to help you work out whether

franchising is for you. They're equally useful for franchisees and
franchisors.

1 **Why do I want to do this?** As with any business, it's
   important to work out why you're doing what
   you're doing and what the main focus of your
   business will be. This will mean you need to have
   real clarity about your work/life goals and balance.
   If you have a partner and family to consider,
   discuss the future with them. Their support will be
   vital: starting a new business, franchise or not, is
   hard work and may include long, unsociable hours.
   Plan time for family discussions and deal with the
   facts that you know about. If family isn't an issue
   for you, it's certainly advisable to run your ideas
   past a trusted friend, colleague or business coach
   as they are likely to know you well and ask
   questions that perhaps you won't ask of yourself. In
   listening to others' views, do keep your ears open
   and give them permission to challenge you as well
   as affirm that they like the idea. You must take on
   board all aspects, without taking offence or
   ignoring negative feedback. Keep your eyes and
   ears wide open.
   As background work for discussions and to develop
   clarity in your mind so that you can make logical

decisions, start making a list of why you want to franchise the business or become a franchisee. There are some suggested headings below, but make up your own to suit your needs:

- Benefits of this new role for me/my family
- Disadvantages of this new role for me/my family
- Benefits of my existing role for me/my family
- Disadvantages of this role for me/my family
- Why I want to do this (in one sentence)

Start to build a picture of your *raison d'être* and work through it carefully. As you note down the various thoughts that spring to mind, be aware of what excites or drains you about the business and this potential change in your life.

2 **What am I escaping from?** Embarking on a brand new career because you're bored with what you're doing is a common move, but it isn't always the best one. What is it, specifically, that is making you want to move on from your existing role? If it's because your boss annoys you and you don't like complying with his or her demands, why will being a franchisee be any different? If your business has reached a plateau and you think that by expanding it will become more fun and have a new lease of life – beware! Similarly, if your business is

floundering, turning it into a franchising business won't work, as to do that successfully you need a strong existing financial and business model that has been piloted and shown to work well. Franchising your business will be hard work and require a huge amount of time as well as financial commitment. Be honest with yourself when thinking about this particular escape route and discuss it thoroughly with a trusted friend, mentor or business coach.

3 **What are the risks for me?** You are the person who is taking on this new role and who will be ultimately responsible for your own contentment in the workplace. Doing a simple SWOT (strengths, weaknesses, opportunities, threats) analysis will help you towards some self-awareness. It's at this stage that you can address the difficulties and, from your experience of how you operate, make a realistic risk assessment. The risks can come in any form: money, time, loneliness, isolation, family pressures etc. Use the table below to collect together your thoughts and see what patterns emerge, if any. (For a slightly different layout, see Chapter 4.) Use the layout that most helps you collect your thoughts. Talk the SWOT analysis through with your chosen colleague or partner.

Strengths	Weaknesses
Opportunities	Threats

Examples of SWOT factors are listed below.

Strengths include:	high-level service
	my experience
	national network
	family support
	work/life balance
Weaknesses include:	inadequate working capital
	poor management skills
	no experience in this market (this could also be an opportunity)
	loneliness
Opportunities include:	gaps in the market
	changing tastes
	unsatisfied needs
	extending my knowledge of this sector
Threats include:	competitive action
	legislation (red tape)
	market trends
	could get bored at home
	work/life balance

If you think of a threat as an opportunity in disguise, your approach may well change.

4 **What impact will my being a franchisee/franchisor have on my family?** This is a new venture and you can best manage the impact of the change on your life by first working out exactly what results you hope to achieve and how you think you're going to get there. If work/life balance is important to you, write down what that means in terms of time by day, week or month. Obviously you also need to consider the financial implications, and this is where a clear sight of your weekly/monthly expenditure is critical. List all expenses and outgoings (it's important to be realistic) and at least you'll know where you need to be. Your franchise budget will then tell you how long it will take you to get there, thus managing everyone's expectations – self, family, bank manager, franchisor. We cover this in depth in Chapter 5, so turn to p. 93.

5 **What qualifications do I need?** You may need specific qualifications for a franchise. For example, if you can't drive, becoming a driving instructor isn't an easy option. However, many driving instructor franchises will guide you on how to prepare yourself and will probably offer to teach

you to drive – at a cost, obviously. Check with the franchise to ensure you have any desired qualifications and find out what training is offered so that you can learn more as you develop your business. And check with the competition too, finding out what standards the competition works to. You may be committing to training that isn't an industry standard and the franchise isn't as valuable as you are being led to believe. Continuous personal development is all the rage for a very good reason: if you grow, your business grows and you create positive momentum.

6   **What sort of person do I need to be?** First and foremost, you need to be someone who is prepared to work and sell hard. If you're a franchisee, in particular, you'll need plenty of enthusiasm and a genuine desire to succeed in your chosen franchise. You can't escape the reality that no matter how good the support from the franchisor, your success will come as a direct result of *your* effort. If you know you don't work well on your own, running a business from your home is going to be a struggle and may just not be a good idea at all. You will need to be prepared to work within the parameters of the franchisor, so if complying with particular administrative procedures isn't your thing, either

don't do it or employ someone in who can. If you don't like managing people and communicating as part of a team, setting up a national franchise network won't suit you unless you find a manager to do those elements for you. Motivation is a key element in determining if you will be successful in business. Often a franchisor is more interested in your enthusiasm to run a successful business than inhow much in-depth knowledge of a particular industry you have.

7 **How good am I at delegating?** Whether you're a franchisee or franchisor, you'll have a team around you to communicate with and delegate to. If you aren't comfortable trusting others or knowing how to build that trust, learn how to! There are a few traditional reasons why we find it hard to delegate, and at every seminar the same old issues arise:

- It's quicker to do it myself.
- I don't trust someone else to do it the way I'd do it.
- I like doing that job and don't want to pass it on.
- I end up doing it myself anyway.

Being aware of these recurring difficulties is half way to solving them, so keep them in mind when thinking about your own delegating skills. And there's a whole section about how to delegate in Chapter 8.

8 **What qualities do I need?** Many magazines and websites publish 'ideal qualities' to be found in franchisees and I've listed a few of my favourites here. It's by no means an exhaustive list, but identifying positively with some or all of these qualities will show you whether you're likely to be able to operate effectively:

- tenacious
- willing to learn
- good at selling
- prepared to work long hours and under pressure
- having an entrepreneurial background
- able to tolerate uncertainty
- happy to delegate
- self-disciplined
- keen to grow your business
- ready to learn from failure
- unlikely to flinch at taking unpopular decisions
- motivated and passionate

Additional questions for a potential franchisor to consider

What do I want the business to look like in five years' time?

It could be that you have had a great idea and a business

model that has worked very successfully so far, but you may not have considered how things may pan out in the future. However, the responsibility of owning and running a franchise means that you have to start looking ahead. If you know that forward planning isn't one of your stengths, work with a partner who can bring that element to your business. It's very easy to become bogged down with day-to-day detail and forget the bigger picture, so allocate yourself time and space to take out your metaphorical binoculars and look at the horizon, with a colleague or business coach if that is more helpful.

Do I really have to do a pilot? The answer is a resounding 'yes'! *You* may be satisfied with your business, but in order to convince others to join in, you'll need solid proof that it works. Business partners, banks and potential franchisees will all ask searching questions that you need to answer accurately and honestly. Turn to Chapter 4 for more information about pilots.

What's my real motivation to own or create a franchise? Passion? Pride? Ego? External pressure? Or does it just seem like a good idea? Explore this question carefully and honestly. The energy and commitment required to make your business into a franchise is considerable. One person I know who is setting up a franchise has almost given up her social life and has another six months left before she'll see light at the end of the tunnel. Is this a place you want to go? A realistic reflection of what is required, done well at the planning stage, will at least ensure you go into franchising with your eyes open.

Can I develop and sustain relationships with many different personalities? As a franchisor, you will be recruiting, training and motivating a wide variety of people across what could become a wide geographical area. If the thought of this fills you with horror, who will you bring in to run the communication side of the business? Relationship-building is an area you can't afford to ignore.

Am I prepared to share some of my present independence/ success with a set of franchisees? Look at this question very honestly. If you *aren't* prepared to share success, bitterness can easily set in and damage your business. Your vision for growth (if you have one) will identify where you sit with this – the key being that if you don't have a proper idea of where you want to go, it will be difficult to expand.

If I need financial help, am I prepared to share ownership of the business? If you're familiar with the *Dragons' Den* series on television, you will have seen a variety of entrepreneurs bringing ideas to investors in the hope of securing finance in order to develop and grow their business – with varying degrees of success. It's fun to watch the negotiation about how much equity they are prepared to part with in order to secure the finance. How do you feel about sharing your business with an investor, in whatever form they appear?

Key points

- Above all, recognise your strengths and weaknesses.
- Think about your key transferable skills that can support you.
- Consider others who are involved in this decision.
- How much are you prepared to delegate?
- If you don't have short-, medium- and long-term goals, now is the time to set them.

Helpful resources

There are plenty of places to find out more about franchising, the key being to look at independent sources and in more than one place.

NatWest/BFA survey – this has some excellent pointers about what makes a good franchisee and what franchisors are looking for. The partnership has 20 years' experience with these surveys, so the information will be valuable to you. Search for 'franchising' at **www.natwest.com/business**.

British Franchise Association (BFA) – as well as the usual industry benefits of membership, the association offers comprehensive seminars, whether you are considering expanding your business through becoming a franchisor or buying a franchise as a franchisee. Seminars are run across the country and you may be charged a small fee for attending. The BFA is a not-for-profit organisation and, although there is no specific franchise law in the UK, it aims to keep the 'streets clean' by encouraging ethical franchising.

There are also BFA-run franchise exhibitions throughout the year and across the globe. If you've never been to an exhibition, they can be bewildering experiences, with thousands of great ideas in one place and more freebies than you can carry. It's a good idea to attend with a clear idea in your mind of what you want to come away with. Check out **www.thebfa.org**.

Whichfranchise.com – this is the official online partner of the BFA and has an extensive website at **www.whichfranchise.com**.

Franchise Development Services (FDS) – this organisation is there to give advice to individuals or businesses who want to set up a franchise. It has a national network and a helpline you can call for free guidance on 01603 620 301. For a more in-depth meeting you will be charged, but advisors have enormous experience in the world of franchising and will be clear with their recommendations.

Business Link – this has a wealth of information about running your own business, including a very accessible franchise section. See **www.businesslink.gov.uk**.

3
INVESTIGATING THE PROS AND CONS OF A FRANCHISE OPPORTUNITY

'DILIGENCE IS THE MOTHER OF GOOD FORTUNE.'

Benjamin Disraeli

This chapter is most relevant for those looking to buy into a franchise and become a franchisee. As a franchisor, it is helpful to see into the minds of those you will potentially work with, so feel free to read this section – you may pick up some fresh ideas.

So you've decided to buy into a franchise as your next business opportunity, either stand-alone or to supplement your existing business, and you're ready to study the market. Don't be surprised by the size of it – it's a hypermarket! There are plenty of areas to think about and you may find it helpful to break them down into sectors and areas of interest within that sector. This is a shopping expedition, and must be treated as such. You will be buying into a product that will be a large part of your life and work, requiring both time and financial commitments. You've already decided you are personally committed to this venture and have the support of those close to you. Now move on to the commitment you will have to make to your franchisor. In investigating the pros and cons of franchising, ask those already in that business for their experiences and advice. You don't have to do all that they tell you but you can certainly learn from them. There may be pitfalls you hadn't thought about or positive new avenues hitherto not considered as a possibility.

It's worth reviewing the different types of franchise available to you and checking your understanding of the type of franchise you are committing to. Here's a quick summary of the main types:

- **Job franchise** – usually described as low-level investment where the franchisee works in the business.
- **Location franchise** – will operate from fixed premises, and these tend to be an important part of the business operation – for example, a retail outlet where customers visit.

- **Investment franchise** – often more expensive than others and frequently classified alongside job and business franchises for the sake of simplicity.
- **Mobile franchise** – usually a vehicle-operated franchise, which goes out to serve customers. This is the opposite of a location franchise and includes companies such as windscreen replacement and car tuning/cleaning services.
- **Fractional franchise** – where the franchise is only part of the franchisee's interest. This is usually related to premises. A franchise shop within a department store is an example, as are certain types of printing operating out of a print shop.
- **Fast-food franchise** – speaks for itself . . . counter service, self-service and takeaway outlets. This book doesn't specifically cover this area, due to all the associated food hygiene requirements.
- **Joint venture** – where the franchisor shares the cost of set-up with the franchisee and then takes a larger share of ownership. Commonly the franchisor (who may be from overseas) will initiate the idea, contribute the know-how/premises and expect the franchisee to provide some or all of the funds and management. Some larger national opticians operate joint ventures.

■ **Business format franchise** – where the franchisor provides all that is needed, including the total business operating format. They will be involved at the outset and on an ongoing basis. Franchisees have the opportunity to build equity in the business.

There are six key stages to address during your selection process. You may choose to work your way up and down the list throughout the process, but I suggest you need to include all six at some point. There is a whole chapter on finance, which will not be covered here.

1 Filter your options to three or four possibilities.
2 List your selection criteria, including finances and your ability to find the correct funding.
3 Brainstorm with a trusted team.
4 Meet the franchisor(s).
5 Meet the other franchisees.
6 Finalise the legal agreement – decide!

No matter how you came to consider the franchise you are committing to, you should go through the same rigorous investigations. Some of the ways people hear about franchises are listed below, together with comments about those sources.

- **From a friend already involved in the franchise.** There's nothing like a personal recommendation, but beware: what's great for them and their lifestyle may not work for you.

- **At a franchise exhibition.** These are great places to start gauging the culture of the business and the people you could be working alongside. You will see a wide variety of options available to you at these events, but remember that not all franchisors take exhibition stands, so you may miss a key company in the sector you are investigating if you restrict your research to them alone. Franchisors investing in exhibition space are certainly keen to be seen by prospective franchisees, and the razzmatazz and freebies on offer can be quite overwhelming, so it's worth preparing well beforehand in order to avoid the 'kid in a sweet shop' syndrome. Bring a list of searching questions to ask exhibitors and then listen carefully to what is said, as well as to what is left unsaid.

- **A franchise magazine.** These are loaded with advertisements for a wide variety of franchises – often by the same people who take exhibition stands. You can sift through the variety of companies and mark the ones you want to follow up.

- **Franmatch.** This is a relatively new matchmaking service for prospective franchisees. They match you with franchisors who suit your requirements, location, suitability . . . and wallet. It is a free service funded by franchisors and you can find more about it on the FDS website.

- **A Web search.** You'll certainly see which franchises have put together an effective website. If you have to trawl through to page 110 to find them, is that where you want your new business to appear? It's a great place to start your search as you'll get a feel for how the company communicates with its customers and franchisees.

- **Word of mouth.** Your existing networks may point you in a direction, but you do need to check that the information is trustworthy with some thorough research.

- **Press articles.** You may read case histories in the local or national press. Check to see if the small print says 'advertorial', 'sponsored by' or similar wording, which means that the company has paid to tell its story. If it's a good journalistic piece, learn from it and follow up as appropriate.

- **Advertisements in newspapers.** There are hundreds of these every week. There's no harm in looking to see what's on the market, but take time to

investigate credentials of 'small ad' companies.
Some businesses, labelled as franchises, aren't.
Use trusted sources such as the BFA to find out if
they are members and at what level. There are
several levels of membership to the BFA: Full,
Associate, Provisional and Exhibition accredited.
Full and Associate members have to prove they
have a viable business that is ethical, disclosed and
transferable. Full members also have to have a
proven trading and franchising record. The BFA
definitions of the criteria are as follows:

Viable: *The business to be franchised must be
viable. Evidence will show that the product or
service is saleable, and at a level of profit that will
sustain a franchised network.*

Transferable: *There is a means for the transfer
of the know-how to a new operator at arm's
length, essential if the business is to be
franchised.*

Ethical: *The franchise is structured and operated
in accordance with the ethical principles set out
in the European Code of Ethics for Franchising,
which covers matters of advertising, recruiting,
selecting and dealing with franchisees. The
applicant's franchise agreement is formally
assessed.*

Disclosed: *All information on the business that is material to the franchise proposition and contract is disclosed without ambiguity to prospective franchisees.*

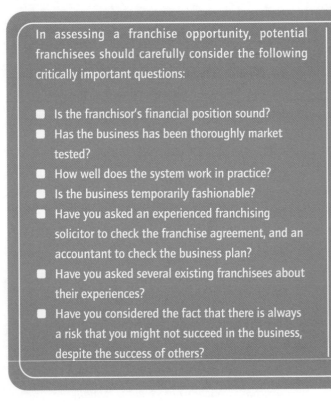

In assessing a franchise opportunity, potential franchisees should carefully consider the following critically important questions:

- Is the franchisor's financial position sound?
- Has the business has been thoroughly market tested?
- How well does the system work in practice?
- Is the business temporarily fashionable?
- Have you asked an experienced franchising solicitor to check the franchise agreement, and an accountant to check the business plan?
- Have you asked several existing franchisees about their experiences?
- Have you considered the fact that there is always a risk that you might not succeed in the business, despite the success of others?

Working through the six stages

Stage 1 – Filter down your options

Whatever your source, you need to filter down to three or four contenders from a variety of categories. If you are coming at this from a completely fresh start with no preconceived ideas about what you want to do, your selections may be across two or three categories. Now's the time to be creative and ask the 'why not?' question – you may find an exciting new niche for yourself. The list on the following page comes from the UK franchise directory. You may find it helpful to cross off the ones you know you won't be pursuing. This is your opportunity to think hard about moving into a new market, if that is the challenge you want. As you trawl through the categories, note the ones that raise your levels of interest, reminding yourself that you need to be really motivated to become a franchisee.

Once you have a few categories to work from, you need to find some specific franchise businesses in those categories. A great first place to start is the UK franchise directory (owned by FDS), where you can sort by investment level, business category, place of operation, franchise type and franchise name. You'll be able to look at the criteria sought by the franchisor and the opportunity they offer, as well as to confirm their BFA membership. If you already know the franchise you're interested in, have a look at their entry and credentials in the

Agriculture	Automotive	Beauty	Beverages
Business to business	Care	Chemical	Children & babies
Cleaning	Communications	Computers	Construction
Consultancy	Customisation	Dating	Delivery
Distribution	Education/ training	Electrical	Entertainment
Environmental	Estate agents	Fashion	Financial
Food	Footwear	Franchise consultants	Garden
Health	Hire	Horticulture	Indoor property
Internet	Investment	Legal	Luxury
Manufacture	Outdoor property	Personal	Pets & animals
Photography	Print & design	Promotional	Recruitment
Repair & maintenance	Retail	Safety	Sales
Security	Services	Signs	Sports
Storage	Supplies	Travel	Used goods

directory. You may have some preconceived ideas that are not based upon facts.

Once you've found some interesting-sounding businesses, search for more detailed information from websites, company brochures, your experience of their outlets, a franchise exhibition and all the other places available to you. Each business should have a franchise prospectus, which should contain some or all of the following information:

- description of the franchise
- directors and key executives
- company track record
- initial investment required
- other payments that will become due to the franchisor
- information on how to raise finance
- any restrictions on franchisee's participation
- termination and renewal of agreement terms
- number and success rates of existing franchisees
- franchisor's rights to select/approve sites
- training and support that the franchisee will be offered (remember to find out how much of this is at an additional cost)
- financial information about the pilot operation (remember, you are looking for a solid business model)

- financial data on the franchisor – feel free to ask for additional data if you think there are glaring omissions
- a list of professional advisors they recommend, as well as the name of the franchisor's banker

With the prospectus and other information you have collected, start to build a picture of the companies you are considering, making a note of your initial responses. They can often be very telling. Are the public areas (reception, waiting rooms, lavatories and so on) well kept, welcoming and tidy? If the small details are attended to, you can bet that will apply across the business. Whether you agree with it or not, first impressions count in many walks of life and this is no exception.

Stage 2 – List your selection criteria

This could be a hugely long list, so beware of confusing yourself. Putting them all in alphabetical order may be useful but it's even better to prioritise what's most important to you. Some suggestions are listed below, but you need to add and prioritise your own criteria for this selection process. Your brainstorming team (see below) may well come up with some criteria not otherwise considered. By completing each section for Companies A, B & C (and so on, depending on how many you've shortlisted) based on your initial experience, a picture may start to emerge and you can either drop one company

Criteria	Company A	Company B	Company C
Culture/ethics			
Credentials/years as franchisor			
Territory			
Customer experience			
Marketing materials			
Full member of the BFA			
Website accessibility			
Training quality			
Training costs			
Flexible hours			
Anticipated break-even			
Investment level			
Monthly fees			
Long-term support			
Research & development			
↓	↓	↓	↓

from your list, or see all three but decide to ask some additional questions of the apparently weaker company.

This is your first filter, and you may well have filtered ten companies down to three or four with a view to investigating them all more fully. This is no bad thing, as websites, glossy brochures and friendly sales patter can be misleading.

Stage 3 – Brainstorm with a trusted team

If you think you'd rather complete the selection process on your own, I'd urge you to reconsider. Successful businesses operate with a strong team and you can practise this with your trusted friends/colleagues. The ultimate decision is of course yours, but no one person has access to all the best ideas and questions. Choose your brainstorming team carefully: they need to be people whose wisdom you respect and who know you well. They must be prepared to have an open mind, to listen as well as offer suggestions, and to put their personal agendas on the back burner for the duration of the brainstorming. It can be tough asking people for their unvarnished opinions rather than having your own thoughts confirmed by a bunch of 'yes' men (or women), so you'll need to select brave brainstormers! Having a small, trustworthy team around you will enhance your confidence and ability to make good, lasting decisions. Explain the situation to everyone, briefing them about your overall objectives, selection criteria and the process/timings you are working to. Thank them for their involvement and, as with any other meeting, set the ground rules. These are the ones I find helpful:

- What is discussed within these four walls is confidential.
- Each of us has the right to be heard.
- Please let me know about ideas that spring to mind after the meeting.
- Please give me 'a gift' by being honest. If you think I'm about to make the biggest mistake of my life, tell me!

It's important to let your brainstorming team know what you are asking of them in terms of time for meetings and your time plan for selecting a franchise. No-one wants to be strung along for months with no outcome.

Stage 4 – Meet the franchisor

You're now ready to take an objective view of the franchises you are considering. Whether you're meeting the franchisor in person or over the phone, find out the franchisee selection criteria and what's important/vital to the franchisor. Any franchisors worth their salt will want to see that you are serious, so prepare well for your meeting and don't be embarrassed about asking lots of questions. Similarly, be open to some searching questions from the franchisor. Your track record is likely to be critical to their selection of you, so bring numbers to support your arguments. If you have positive customer case histories, these will be helpful. Point the franchisor to your website, if you have one.

This part of your investigation is a bit like an interview, where you're sizing one another up for what you both hope will be a long-term, successful business relationship. Listen carefully, look out for non-verbal cues in the other person's body language, keep up confident eye contact and watch out for all the things you'd notice when meeting a potential business partner. In addition to the practical questions about investment and so on that you have come up with in your table, I've shown below some of the things you can look out for. Even if they aren't direct questions, it is all information that will be helpful. For example, as part of my research for this book I went along to a driving school open meeting, where they explained how to become a driving instructor. They were very friendly and helpful, but any questions that did not relate directly to teaching people to drive couldn't be answered. The person who dealt with territories and agreements wasn't in the office that day. I was a little suspicious, as the newspaper ad had said 'Find out all about . . .', when clearly that wasn't possible. I turned to generic questions about how many instructors they have and how long these stay as franchisees. The answer clearly showed high turnover after the first year. So that wouldn't have been the place for me to build a long-term relationship. The flat monthly fee with little incentive for growth was another negative pointer for me.

Whatever you do, think on your feet. There is usually more than one way to find the information you are looking for. Two heads are better than one, so I suggest you meet the franchisor with one of your support team whose strengths cover your weaker spots. An accountant, for example, would see an angle that an optimistic sales person may miss. Here are some generic questions and types of questions to ask, or at least to bear in mind.

- What does the British Franchise Association (BFA) say about this franchise? Is the company a member of the BFA?
- What is this franchisor's corporate social responsibility policy?
- How long has the franchise been operating? Do they have a positive track record?
- What experience have I had of this franchise as a consumer?
- Have any of my friends experienced this franchise as a consumer?
- How important is regular contact with the franchisor?
- Will I be expected to attend regular meetings a long way from home?

- How much does gut instinct and trust come into my selection of a franchise?
- Who owns the franchisor's business?

Before any meeting, also remember to:

- include any questions related to your key criteria
- find out about any operating restrictions – your entrepreneurial spirit may be stunted and the franchise wouldn't suit you
- delve into the prospectus and ask follow-up questions
- look on franchising websites for a selection of questions to consider
- review Chapter 8 (What to do if things go wrong) to see some of the warning signs of a franchise to avoid

During your meeting, it's also essential to remember that this is a two-way street. Keen as you are to find out about the franchisor, they will also want to establish your viability as a franchisee. There may be hot competition, with one franchisee to find from 40 to 50 potential candidates. A franchisor must protect their brand and quality of delivery and it follows that they will want to pick a winner from amongst the candidates. Some franchisors may ask you to complete a personality type indicator test in order to help with their selection process. Compatibility is essential for a successful business relationship. If your desire to make money is hidden from view and they need tough sales people with a real desire to make large profits, why would they select you as a franchisee? Do find out the franchisor's 'hot' buttons , if you can, and bring information and questions to hit those buttons.

Having met the franchisor and asked your questions, start to complete your filter sheet (see overleaf for an example). Your picture is building and you can sort the list to suit your brief. Watch a pattern emerging. In this example, an investment of £150,000 may be out of your reach so you can narrow the list down to two pretty quickly.

Stage 5 – Meet the franchisees

A major part of your investigation of the pros and cons of a franchise opportunity is to meet other, existing franchisees. First you have to find them, and the franchisor is the one to ask. Be wary if the franchisor is evasive about full lists of franchisees; they should willingly give you a list of people to speak to. You could ask for a list that includes a variety of franchise experiences – for example the most successful, longest relationship, the most recent joiner, fastest growing franchise etc. It's also important to ask the franchisor and franchisees what elements contribute to less successful franchises and what lessons can be drawn from these. Naturally, the 'showcase'

Criteria	Company A	Company B	Company C
Culture/ethics	3/10	9/10	6/10
Credentials/ years as franchisor	6 years	10 years	1 year
Territory	9/10	7/10	10/10
Customer experience	7/10	9/10	8/10
Marketing materials	8/10	10/10	6/10
Website	10/10	8/10	6/10
Training quality	8/10	10/10	5/10
Training costs	£1k year	£included	£included
Flexible hours	Unlikely	Eventually	??
Anticipated break-even	18 months	2 years	12 months
Investment cost	£10K	£20K	£150K
Monthly cost	7% of sales	Flat fee	3%
Long-term support	10/10	9/10	unknown
Research & development	6/10	8/10	3/10
Additional comments:			
↓	↓	↓	↓

franchisees who appear in advertisements or at exhibitions will be running successful businesses and be all too willing to bring you on board. In the real world, though, there are bound to have been some failures or things that haven't gone well for any franchisor/franchisee. Threatening questions about failures will bring little or no response, so rather than seeking out 'horror stories', look for a realistic perspective on how the business has built over time. The following questions will help you to build your picture:

- What was the biggest challenge in your first six months as franchisee?
- How did the franchisor help you in the hard times?
- What were the extra costs you hadn't anticipated?
- You seem to have a fabulous, central territory. How long did it take to secure as part of your agreement?
- What are your long-term ambitions? (Ideally they will they correlate with yours.)
- What would you do differently if you were starting this franchise today?
- How do you source your customers?
- What else do I need to know?

Whatever you do, assure a franchisee of the confidentiality of your questions and their answers. Be quite upfront about why you're meeting them and allow time for them to think and respond. They are giving their valuable time to you – thank them for it.

Stage 6 – Decide!

Armed with a wealth of information, you now need to sit down with it all and, if it isn't already obvious, make your decision. By now you will have identified any risks and be comfortable with them as part of the new venture you are taking on.

Key points

- Does the franchise you are choosing allow you to meet your personal and business goals?
- Ask about long-term support of franchisees and expansion possibilities.
- Allow your trusted brainstorm team to help your thought processes.
- Think about the '3 Cs' – culture, cash and credentials.

Things to watch out for

- Read between the sales lines.
- Understand territorial implications.
- Know how to sell or get out of the franchise agreement.
- Franchises that don't have agreements aren't true franchises.

Helpful resources

The UK Franchise Directory – **www.theukfranchisedirectory.net**

Which Franchise – **www.whichfranchise.com**

Daltons Weekly business section – **www.daltonbusiness.com**

The British Franchise Association (BFA) – **www.thebfa.org.uk**

Franmatch – a subsidiary of FDS, Franmatch assists with matching franchisees to franchisors, see **www.franmatch.com**

4
INVESTIGATING THE PROS AND CONS OF FRANCHISING YOUR BUSINESS

If you feel your business has a model that can act as a template for others, read on! Setting up even the simplest franchise can be expensive, though, so be prepared for this. Don't be tempted to take short cuts, as you'll generally regret your economies. As you proceed with your planning, take good, solid advice from those with relevant experience. If you haven't been a franchisor before, speak to plenty of franchisees about their experiences and what they found helpful from their franchisor. Industrial espionage sounds like something out of a James Bond film, but it's a real issue: you'll need to protect your intellectual property rights by registering trademarks, trade names and patents with the relevant trademark and patent

> offices. Don't give your main competitors a head start when franchising hadn't previously crossed their minds.

From a bright idea will come hundreds of details that fly into your head at all times of the day and night, both the welcome and not-so-welcome. These ideas need to be collected and sifted through as part of your considerations, so choose a method that works during the daytime and won't keep you awake at night. A book and pen by your bedside for 3am thoughts will allow you to get back to sleep. The following six areas will need to be considered as you approach franchising. The last point, about recruiting, training and motivating franchisees, will be covered in more detail in Chapter 8.

1   Decide why you want to franchise your business and what your vision is for it.
2   Test your theory that franchising is a good idea for *your* business.
    ■ Research the market to ensure your product or service is competitive and distinctive enough to be franchised and that customer demand is sufficiently widespread.

■ Produce a business plan outlining proposals in full and include a detailed SWOT analysis.

■ Protect your intellectual property.

3. Set up a pilot, with realistic measurements.

4. Be clear on your financial needs for the pilot and roll-out.

5. Draw up key documents.

6. Recruit, train and motivate franchisees.

Let's look at the areas in more detail.

Area 1 – Decide why you want to franchise your business and what your vision is for it

From the outset, be clear about why you're doing what you're doing. Setting up your own franchise operation will be time-consuming, exciting and at times disheartening. Having that clarity of purpose will keep you on track.

In Chapter 3, we looked at how to build a brainstorming team. While this is your idea, and your first thoughts on vision need to be yours, I suggest, once you are clear in your own mind, that you develop a similar team for your current investigations. Surround yourself with trusted people (not too many), who don't necessarily have vested interests and who will help you to keep sight of your vision. If your purpose for franchising is making money, that's absolutely fine . . . but call it what it is without hiding behind a warm and fuzzy smokescreen of environmental or ethical issues. The vision that you have will need to be communicated to customers and franchisees, so the clearer and easier it is to understand, the better. For help with developing a succinct, marketable vision, you may at a later stage employ a professional marketer. You could invest in one now, but he or she won't be able to give you your vision; that has to come from you. The following questions will help you to start building a picture:

- What does my business do?
- Why do I want others involved in the business?
- At the end of the first year, what do I want my business to look like?
- After five years, what do I want my business to look like?
- What sort of people will the franchisees need to be?

Area 2 – Test your theory that franchising is a good idea for *your* business

Where better to start testing your theory than in the franchise market? If 25 other companies have successfully franchised a similar business to yours, you could be on the right track. That said, you'll need to decide whether you are entering a cluttered market. If you are, are you sufficiently confident in your product being able to rise above that clutter to keep going with your investigations of the pros and cons? Alternatively, have you spotted a gap in the market that your business can fill? Be realistic when thinking about gaps in the market: are you the only person who thinks there's a gap in the market, or do others agree with you? Where will you go to find out? You can take independent advice from a company such as Franchise Development Services (FDS) as a starting point. They have experience in the entire franchise market and will be clear about what can work and what has failed in the past. You don't need to take theirs as the last word, but they will surely point you in a sensible direction.

Before moving further, remind yourself that for your business to be successful as a franchise it needs to be:

- **'Clonable'** – It should be easy to transfer your service/expertise or know-how to franchisees. To establish whether this is the case, explain your franchise idea to a few trusted people as if they were potential franchisees and see how they react. If that glazed look comes over their faces and they 'tune out', either you need to make your model easier to understand, or it is too complicated to be viable at the moment. I've asked a number of people to explain their franchise ideas to me and lost interest pretty quickly due to lack of clarity on their part. You may have plenty of passion about your idea and be able to see it in your mind's eye, but ideas have to come out of your head and be put down on paper – preferably one sheet of A4.

- **Competitive** – What's going to make you attractive to customers and franchisees alike? Why will they want to do business with you and not your competitors?
- **Profitable** – Not only will you be running your own business, but your profit margins will have to support your new franchise activity as a franchisor.
- **Backed by a contingency plan** – The best-laid plans can go off course, for a variety of reasons. Ensure you have finance to support this. (See Chapter 5.)

Once you see that franchising your business is a possibility in principle – that is, there's a vision and a market – you need to look at your business model and plan. A rigorous inspection of the model by your accountant or bank must be a first step, or you could go to a company that specialises in helping businesses to set up franchises, although they may charge you a small fee. Whichever you choose, establish how much this rigorous inspection is going to cost you, and ensure it is a confidential discussion and that you aren't agreeing to anything other than their comments. Going back to *Dragons' Den*, few of the propositions we see on screen are of interest to the investors. If you scratch the surface of a fairly sensational delivery style designed to boost TV audiences, you'll see some of the pretty basic questions contestants are unable to answer:

- How many customers have you had in the past
  12 months?
- How do customers hear about your product?
- What's your annual turnover?
- How much profit did you make in the past
  12 months?
- How many customers do you need to break even on
  this investment?
- What's your budget for research and development?
- What makes you different from any other company
  selling this product?

These are all the sorts of questions you must be able to answer when testing your theory that your business model can become a successful franchise operation.

From one of the high street banks[2], I read research showing that for businesses which don't plan, average profits are 35% – a decent return. Compare that with businesses planning regularly, where profits averaged 54%. Over 50% more profit just because of some regular planning – it's a no-brainer!

If you've never planned before, seek professional advice. Most high street banks and accountants will have some kind of business planning tool you can use and they are likely to be

2 Barclays

quite in-depth. But there's plenty you can do to prepare for such a meeting. Start simply, in order to keep the vision of your business idea in focus. Use a format to suit your style such as a mind map, a list or a spreadsheet, and include the following headings:

- aims of the business
- objectives
- resources available
- projected costs
- projected revenue streams
- staff requirements
- finding customers/franchisees
- premises
- franchisee feedback

As described on page 28, a SWOT analysis is an extremely useful tool to aid understanding and decision-making in all sorts of situations in business and organisations. Completing a SWOT analysis is very simple, and is best done with a small group in order to consider all the options – your trusted team will help you with this. You can adapt the style below, as long as you take time to work through your business with an eye on the competition and the outside world. I've put in a few ideas to show how the SWOT picture can be built.

STRENGTHS	WEAKNESSES
Experience	Limited franchisee
Committed team	sources
Business model	Travel costs
Marketing	Detracts from existing
Unique selling point	business
Staff	Trademark protection

OPPORTUNITIES	THREATS
Distribution	Competition
Profit	Franchisee selection
Brand building	errors
	Finance

Once complete, have a look at the threats and see how it changes your perspective when you view a threat as an opportunity.

Once you have a clear business plan and SWOT analysis, you are in a better position to seek independent advice with confidence. When you meet the person advising you, such as your bank manager, keep an open mind if he or she asks probing questions. The temptation, when lacking in confidence or answers, is to close down or come out fighting by challenging such questions. A good independent advisor will want to help you, so their questions are for the most professional of motives. By all means ask what lies behind the question, and listen carefully to the answers. But whoever you work with at this stage could well be a longer-term partner, so this is a time to establish boundaries and learn to work well together. Employ all your best listening skills and learn from what you hear. Take notes that will help you with your decision-making at a later stage and, of course, ask for clarification of jargon.

It's also important at this stage to protect your intellectual property (IP). While this may sound a little drastic so early in your thoughts about becoming a franchisor, do you really want to reach the end of a long investigation process and pilot to discover that you either can't use a name or someone else has taken it in the meantime? Intellectual property covers your secrets of doing business and various trademarks, branding, manuals etc., all of which should be legally protected before being sold in a franchise package. A serious franchisee will ask about intellectual property, as they won't want to buy into a franchise that doesn't really exist or won't be able to trade. The area of intellectual property must be handled through a lawyer if you are to be sure of your security. The BFA website has a list of professional advisors you can approach, and you must be convinced whoever you use has experience in the franchise market. Find out how much you will be charged to secure your intellectual property and remember to add those costs to your list of investments in the business. Check out how long the IP lasts for and if there are any ongoing costs.

Area 3 – Set up a pilot, with realistic measurements

Virtually every business start-up plan has to be changed during the first months of implementation – as proved by the fact that there are high rates of business failure, particularly after the first 30 months of trading[3]. By moving into the franchise business rather than expanding your own team, you're effectively starting a new business and thus entering new, potentially dangerous waters. There is much at stake for you and your franchisees. Even the least expensive franchise system may cost £50,000 in development costs. Diving into shark-infested waters isn't helpful, so it's essential to check before taking the plunge. A pilot is there to confirm whether your business model can be franchised. It will also tell you whether franchising is in fact the best option. You must therefore be ready to accept your findings and may well need to manage your disappointment should your idea fail to work as you had hoped. Your trusted team of advisors will play an important part in the pilot, and you may also find it helpful to use a project management tool. You may find that your existing computer software includes one, but if not, there are plenty on the

3 Lloyds TSB

market. Whatever you decide, you need to be 100% organised for your pilot.

Your pilot operation needs to last at least 12 months – ideally longer if the business is in any way seasonal. If you have a long-established business which is profitable, you may decide to let this represent your pilot. But beware of short cuts in this area. Your franchise will be relying upon third parties to succeed, and you won't have tested this when running your own business. It may not be immediately obvious why your business is doing well. For example, a restaurant – is it successful because of:

- the location
- the food
- the manager's social skills
- the ambience
- the prices
- or something else?

So, the first purpose of the pilot is to find out what makes the business succeed before you think about replicating it elsewhere.

The pilot scheme should be undertaken at more than one location in order to test the concept in different geographical areas as well as other success factors that you have identified. A comprehensive pilot operation will prove the viability of strategy and approach, highlight problem areas, and enable you, the franchisor, to fine-tune the package before committing fully to developing a network. For information on the nuts and bolts of running the pilot, see Chapter 6.

Measuring what you've done

Once you've worked out the practicalities of setting up your pilot, you need to decide how you're going to measure whether it works or not. Not only are you managing your own business, but adding franchisees to the mix. What you measure will depend upon your type of business, but in all cases will need to include clear, financial outcomes. This is where clarity in your business plan – along with a well-defined vision of what success 'looks like' – will be invaluable, as you will know which elements are important. Some of the areas to measure could be as listed below. This isn't an exhaustive list, of course, but gives you some thoughts to start the ball rolling. Add your own where applicable.

- training
- information technology (IT)
- communication with franchisees
- customer complaints
- payment systems
- marketing/launch
- profit

- property
- work/life balance
- staffing levels and quality
- expenses/costs

Don't be shy about adding areas for measurement that others suggest but you hadn't considered: you want to be absolutely sure that your business will work well as a franchise. Do be sure that the measurements you take are relevant in building a picture of whether franchising is the right direction for your business.

Once you've completed the list of *which* areas to measure, you need to work out *how* you will measure them. For example:

- **Training**. If you have built in a two-day training programme, was that sufficient? What would have worked better and how does that affect your profitability? How much extra did the training cost you/the franchisee?
- **IT**. Did the new programme run at the required capacity levels? If there were out-of-hours problems, how were they handled? Weekly sales numbers – was receipt of these often enough, or do you need to know each day?
- **Communication with franchisees**. Are they driving you mad by phoning every two minutes with

questions? If they are, you will need to consider whether your training and manual should be reviewed to answer their questions in a more accessible format.

Look at the pattern of questions: are any trends emerging? Are all the questions on the same theme? If they are, you will need to adapt your manual and/or training programme.

A 12-month pilot scheme must be reviewed regularly. Besides checking your agreed measurements, you need to put milestones in place that allow for a formal review with parties you trust. Be careful not to micro-manage a pilot operation: if you don't let the franchisee operate independently and keep breathing down his or her neck every two minutes, you have to ask whether your business is truly replicable. It MUST be able to run without you on the premises or on the phone 'fire-fighting' all the time. Be prepared to make changes along the way, but do be careful that you don't simply jump at the behest of any franchisee who suggests improvements. Build in a system for franchisee feedback and involve them in your reviews, if you think that will be helpful. You'd be amazed how many companies suffer from 'meeting mania', where meetings happen and nothing much is achieved or agreed. If you aren't used to conducting meetings, there are a few simple steps you can take to increase their effectiveness.

1 Agree date, time and venue of meeting. Ensure all parties will have access to the venue and that they know the anticipated end time of the meeting. Supply directions and details about parking/public transport, if appropriate.

2 Let attendees know who will be there and how they fit into the picture. Preparation is key to meetings, and people are more likely to be at their ease if they know how many and who will be attending.

3 Put together an agenda for the meeting. It can be as simple as this:

REVIEW MEETING – AGENDA

The key theme for the meeting is 'Success for everyone!' The questions we will address are as follows: What is going well? What hasn't gone so well? What could work better and how can we work together to ensure success?

0930	Welcome & introductions
1000	Franchisor presentation of vision and month 1 findings
1030	Question & answer session
1100	Comfort break
1115	Franchisee 1 & 2 presentations, including questions
1200	Success for everyone. Looking ahead to months 2 and 3

<blockquote>

1300	Lunch
1400	Training update and review of manual
1530	Tea and close

Individual franchisee meetings that have been requested will happen after tea. Please book your slot in advance.

Copies of all presentations will be available for you to take away.

</blockquote>

Your agenda will set the pace for the future so think carefully about how you want to run the meetings and use a template that manages expectations. (By that, I mean that people must know what they need to think about before the meeting as well as what to bring with them.) Running a meeting as well as contributing to it can be difficult and not altogether productive, so think about asking a facilitator to run the meeting on your behalf, briefing them fully on your expectations and requirements. Perhaps one of your trusted team of advisors would be willing to do this, or a business coach, if you have one, would be ideally equipped as a facilitator.

4   If you want people to prepare anything specific for the review meeting, ask them in writing, being clear about your expectations. 'Please present for

15 minutes on the key source for your new customers and how you make the most of your local networks. If you will be using PowerPoint, please send the presentation to me by 3pm the day before we meet. Please provide a one-page summary of your recommendations for each attendee. Thank you for offering to do this.' You will want to review their presentation to ensure it meets the brief and will add to the meeting.

5 On the day of the meeting, arrive in good time. You should already have briefed the venue about your requirements for the day, including flip charts, pens, IT, food etc. Be ready to welcome those attending and make them feel at their ease.

6 During the meeting, keep to time and focus on the agenda items. Listen for weasel words that don't give concrete facts such as 'probably', 'maybe' and 'potentially'. Are you living in the real world or hoping for the best with nothing specific to justify this? If new issues arise that take you off the track of the agenda, you could seek agreement from the group to have an 'Any other business' session after tea, though this can really only work if everyone can be involved. An alternative is to note the new items and put them on the agenda for the next meeting, as it's only a month away. Either way, be

sure you leave the meeting with your main agenda items addressed.

7   Follow up wisely. The world is full of places where meetings are held for meetings' sake and progress either isn't made, or is extremely slow and/or painful. Be sure that your meetings close with verbal agreement of what will happen next and who is responsible for which area. Then follow this up with written confirmation for all attendees to see. This isn't red tape gone mad – it's a new business that must run well with everyone taking responsibility for their action points. Writing a follow-up note allows for failing memories to be jogged and offers a point of reference for the next review meeting.

Your review meetings will enable you to establish the progress of the pilot, make changes where helpful and review those changes at the next meeting. Only when the pilot operation is running successfully can you prepare and launch the network.

Area 4 – Be clear on your financial needs for the pilot and roll-out

As a franchisor you will need to commit substantial amounts of time and money before your income stream begins – for market research studies, pilot schemes, promotional material explaining the benefits of the franchise to potential franchisees, the selection and training of franchisees, the production of an operations manual, the formation of a central management team, initial stock and equipment, the launch of the franchise network and advertising. Talk to your accountant and bank to discuss the best way to handle the finances. Generally there's more than one way to skin a cat, so look at all the options and find the one that works the best for your business. Perhaps you have private investors who will invest in your business, but don't be taken in by what sounds like an easy option of money offered to you by family or friends. Agreements with them must be as watertight as with a bank and investigated just as thoroughly. A nod, wink or handshake aren't enough, even if they seem like a good idea at the time.

However you decide to fund your franchise pilot and business, you will need to have your business plan and SWOT analysis in place so you have something to show potential investors. Keep it simple to start with by explaining the big idea and your vision for the business. Top-line figures of the investment you are seeking and a simple calculation, to show you know what you're talking about and where you are going, will give a potential investor confidence in you. Fuzzy explanations with no clear financial facts won't do because, to put it bluntly, investors want to make money out of you. As well as your business model inspiring confidence, you must do the same. If you are clear with your initial presentation, potential investors are more likely to be interested and ask you to expand upon the detail.

Good investors will support you in your venture in order to protect and maximise their investment. It's wise to shop around for investors as they will be with you for some time. As with the rest of your business, think about your culture and the credentials of your potential investors. An interfering relative may not be what you need in a new business venture, however experienced (or wealthy) they are! Banks often make the best investors because they can help you and offer a variety of services. And don't forget that, even though you're asking them to invest, you can still negotiate a deal. After all, you have a great idea that will make money for both sides. Banks recognise that franchising is a relatively secure trading environment and, if you develop a good working relationship, will be able to advise your potential franchisees about investment too. Building a strong relationship with your investors is important as the business develops. Chapter 5 has more specific detail about investing in the franchise business.

Area 5 – Draw up key documents

There are some essential documents that need to be put together before you can recruit franchisees. You cannot take your business to potential franchisees without an operating manual in place, for example.

Operating manual

This reinforces the terms and conditions of the franchise agreement, provides the franchisee with information about working methods and practices, and sets out the way in which the franchise must be operated. If you think about visiting a franchised fast food restaurant, anywhere in the UK, the colour scheme and method of operating are exactly the same. The Stagecoach Theatre Arts plc insists on exact paint colours, look and feel to their venues so that the same customer experience extends globally. So as you prepare your operating manual, cover every item down to the last detail. You are building your brand, and the manual will allow the effective set-up and support of your franchise business. Short cuts in this area will cost you dearly in the long term, as loopholes and misunderstandings will arise almost immediately.

In summary, the operating manual will:

- set and enable you to maintain quality standards
- impose conformity across the developing network
- incorporate means for monitoring and control
- set benchmarks for continuous improvement

It must therefore be designed to be used as:

- a training tool:
    - for the franchisor at induction training, or when

operating at arm's length (i.e. in local offices/
territories)
- for the franchisee when training staff
- a marketing tool
- a sales development tool

Be sure that the manual is easy and cost-efficient to update. And don't send it out to potential franchisees. By all means, let them view the manual in your presence (if you think they are genuine) but you *must* be careful that it doesn't fall into the hands of a potential competitor. A more detailed explanation on how to put together the manual is included in Chapter 6.

The franchise agreement

This sets out the legal obligations of the franchisor and franchisee (Chapter 6 covers this in more detail). You will not be able to recruit franchisees or begin a pilot until you have your agreement in place. It needs to work in tandem with the operating manual for maximum clarity, and must be drawn up by a lawyer familiar with the franchising business. A list of such lawyers can be found on the BFA website and in many of the franchising magazines and websites. Take time to find the right lawyer for yourself and your business and, of course, find out about initial and ongoing costs. Be sure to know what you will be charged for and when payments will be due, and add these costs into your financial planning.

Franchise prospectus

Once you have decided what franchisees will be buying, you need to prepare a prospectus. This tells them what you are offering and what they can expect – it's a sales and marketing tool. Chapter 3 gives a suggested list of items to include, and you can also find information about what to include from a whole host of websites, including the BFA's and Franchise Advice. Your lawyer will be able to advise you too, as will your accountant for the financial elements. Bear in mind that you are likely to be competing with other businesses to attract potential franchisees, which means you need to show clearly your point of difference or unique selling point (USP). At the same time, think carefully about what kinds of people you want to apply (see Chapter 6). Among other things, they will need to have the finances to invest in the business, and the right management skills and attitude. Think: Cash – Culture – Credentials.

Area 6 – Recruit, train and motivate franchisees

On average it takes a franchisee five months to decide to purchase a franchise and a further two months to be trained and set up in business. Therefore it can take a new franchisor up to seven months to recruit their first franchisee. From the Natwest/BFA survey 2007.

Be careful when looking for pilot franchisees that you don't undersell your franchise. It will be tempting to offer discounts in order to secure people willing to take a risk with your pilot, but I suggest you think of it differently – perhaps under the following headings:

- I have a good proposition.
- I am prepared to wait to find the right franchisees.
- What benefits can I offer as part of running the pilot, e.g. extra training?
- What advantages are there to being the first through the door with the pilot?
- I need the initial franchise fee – how can I afford to reduce it?
- The ongoing fee must be right because I'll never be able to raise the levels in the future.
- Could I defer some payments from the franchisee?
- What will future franchisees say if fees are all variable?
- I must be consistent.

Take good time to research your pilot and find the right franchisees. Once the network is up and running, the franchisor and the central management team need to constantly monitor the performance of the outlets, to ensure that quality levels are maintained and to identify and assist any franchisees who are in difficulties. A franchisor's ongoing commitment, through training, product development and other support, is vital to the success of the franchise network.

You are going to be responsible for driving your business, so you'll need to decide if you will handle the day-to-day management of people and systems or whether you will employ someone to do it on your behalf. As discussed above, to recruit franchisees you will need to produce a suitable prospectus, a comprehensive operations manual and a training programme for franchisees. This will enable you, the franchisor, to set and maintain standards of customer service throughout the network. Recruiting the right franchisees can take up to seven months, and they won't run themselves. You will have to:

- establish a central management function, possibly employ field staff to support the franchise network, and set up a system to monitor the performance of franchisees
- develop a marketing, sales and advertising strategy to promote the franchise network, especially when competing with rival companies, so that potential customers are fully aware of the services on offer

The people you select to buy franchises are the ones who are going to assist in the growth of your business as a brand.

Culture will play an important part in your selection, as will financial and business acumen. Before meeting and recruiting potential franchisees you must find them. Lloyds TSB conducted some research with franchisors at a UK franchise exhibition, asking about the cost of recruiting franchisees. It showed that the average was between £3,000 and £10,000 for each franchisee recruited. It should be noted that a higher percentage of long-established franchisors reported that their recruitment costs were at the upper end of the scale.

The BFA's annual survey showed that franchisees took a range of actions prior to acquiring a franchise. The three most popular were: checking franchisor's website, buying a BFA information pack and attending a franchise exhibition. Surprisingly (I think) seminars, extended family and the trade press received no first-choice selections. As a franchisor you can begin to see how important it is to have a professional website and to beware of spending a fortune on trade press. And with exhibition stands coming in the top three places franchisees look, you should expect to invest in that area. Shop around for the price of stands – they vary dramatically in what you get for your money – and beware of paying for bells and whistles that don't add value to anything other than your ego.

You will need to develop a selection process that works for you. It could look something like this but you need to adapt it to suit your franchise:

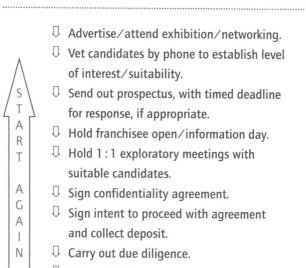

- ⇩ Advertise/attend exhibition/networking.
- ⇩ Vet candidates by phone to establish level of interest/suitability.
- ⇩ Send out prospectus, with timed deadline for response, if appropriate.
- ⇩ Hold franchisee open/information day.
- ⇩ Hold 1 : 1 exploratory meetings with suitable candidates.
- ⇩ Sign confidentiality agreement.
- ⇩ Sign intent to proceed with agreement and collect deposit.
- ⇩ Carry out due diligence.
- ⇩ Set up training programme.
- ⇩ Launch.

As you develop your franchise business, you are likely to become more discerning when spotting the difference between serious requests and casual enquiries. Some franchisor websites have their outline prospectus online, with a separate page for frequently asked questions. They then offer the opportunity to make contact more formally. This can work well as long as your website is 100% functional and professionally laid out. If you are losing potential franchisees at this first hurdle, you need to improve your website to make it more user-friendly.

Once people have expressed an interest in your franchise, you will need to decide whether you want to meet them one-to-one first, or invite them to an open day for a number of potential franchisees. If you go for the open day option, make sure it's well structured and maximises the time you and potential franchisees have to gather all the information needed. Such a day will take a lot of organisation if it is to be professionally delivered. With your presentation, answer core questions about your franchise potential. Examples of the sort of areas people will ask about are:

Legalities
- When do I have to sign the agreement?
- Do I need to pay for a lawyer or is it self-explanatory?
- How long does the agreement last and do I have to pay for a renewal?

Investment
- How much investment is needed?
- How long will it be until my business is profitable?
- Do you supply an accounts system/accountant?

Sales
- Do you generate sales leads?
- What if I've never done any selling before?
- What about existing customers – do I keep them?

Territory

- What if I can't get the territory I want?
- Do I have to live in my territory?
- Can I have more than one territory?

Training

- Is training included in the fees?
- I've been a plumber all my life; do I still need to do your training?
- Who trains the staff I employ?

Marketing

- I've built my own website. Can I have my own page on yours?
- Can I design my own advertising?
- Who pays for the advertising?

Deliver with clarity, honesty and supporting numbers that don't baffle. You are setting the tone for your brand and will need to sell the benefits of franchising, and your franchise option in particular. Listen carefully to the questions being asked, as they can reveal much about the questioner.

When recruiting, it will be a real temptation to select people who are like you, but complementary abilities and weaknesses are the way to go, rather than duplicating yours. The other temptation is to use your instinct or gut feelings.

However, if things go wrong, you will then have to accept the limitations of your personal selection. To avoid these temptations, take a measured approach to the selection process, ensuring you have standard questions for each applicant.

In summary

To summarise, think about the following benefits and disadvantages of becoming a franchisor:

Benefits

Growth

Growing your business can be difficult and expensive. The more you grow, the more capital you need, for example, to finance new outlets. At the same time, managing the business becomes more difficult, particularly if it is spread across the country. Franchising helps overcome these two problems.

As your business grows through franchising, there can be additional benefits. The more franchisees you have, the better-known your brand becomes. Your purchasing power may also increase as you buy more, allowing you to negotiate discounts.

Finance

Each franchisee finances their own outlet themselves. While the franchisee meets all the costs and collects the income, you receive franchise fees from them. You may also make money from supplier mark-ups. You must ensure your finances are planned realistically.

Management demands

The franchisees also run their businesses themselves, reducing the management demands placed on you. Instead, your role involves supporting them. The best franchisees will be highly motivated and have local expertise, making your life much easier.

Potential drawbacks

You need to invest in developing and marketing the franchise. You also need to make sure that you find the right franchisees and control what they do. A bad franchisee can damage your reputation, hurting all your franchisees and your overall brand.

Setting up a franchise is extremely time-consuming and can cost up to £50,000 for the smallest of operations. If, having read this chapter, you still want to franchise your business – congratulations! It's a big step to take and can be an exciting venture. Stay focused!

Key points

- Keep your sights fixed on your vision for the business.
- A robust business model is essential.
- Build a support base of trusted people.

- Be prepared for the pilot to show where changes need to be made.

Things to watch out for

- Not developing your idea in enough depth.
- Asking too many people for their opinions, thereby causing confusion.
- You will need more time and money than you think to set up a franchise business.

Helpful resources

- *Steps to Success: Manage projects successfully*
  ISBN 978-0-7136-8154-3
- Meeting facilitation – www.cliftonconsulting.com

5 HOW MUCH DO I NEED TO INVEST IN THE FRANCHISE BUSINESS?

The question of how much you need to invest in the franchise business is about your time as well as the money involved, whether you are a franchisee or franchisor. If you want to invest every day of the next six months in a franchise business, that's fine, but it must fit in with the rest of your life and cash flow. When it comes to money and investment, you must look at the facts rather than simply saying optimistically that 'it'll all work out fine somehow'.

According to the 2008 Natwest/BFA survey on finance and franchises:

■ The average initial outlay for setting up a franchise is £45,400, though this varies from sector to sector.

- Banks are the most important overall source of finance. Around half of franchisees borrowed money to set up. Of these, 82% borrowed from banks (92% when loans were for more than £20,000).
- The average amount borrowed, by those that did so, was £50,500 (including fees, salaries and all business costs), up from £29,500 in 1992.
- The average ongoing management service fee and advertising levy is 7.5% and 3% of franchisee's turnover respectively.

If you are moving from paid employment to become a franchisee, you need to take a keen interest in the financing of your business. Your monthly salary cheque is no longer guaranteed, and it can take a while to get used to working in this new, less secure fashion. That's why it's vital for you to be surrounded by professional advisors who know exactly how to support you and your business. Some of the terminology may be a mystery to you – learn what it all means so your eyes can stay wide open. There are a few basic terms here, and you can find more on the Business Link website:

Balance sheet – a financial statement at a given point in time. It provides a snapshot summary of what a business owns or is owed (assets) and what it owes (liabilities).

Budget – a plan specifying how a company's resources will be spent or allocated during a particular period

Capital – money invested in a business

Cash flow – the movement of money through a business that is generated by its own operations rather than by borrowing. Cash flow is made up of the money received by sales (cash inflow) and the money spent (cash outflow).

Credit reference agency – used by banks to check people's identity and credit history when they apply for credit. The information provided includes whether they are a voter at the address they provided (this means they'll be on the electoral register), whether they have failed to repay debts, or whether they have been taken to court for not paying back a debt. Everyone is allowed to see their own records.

Gross – total, before consideration of taxes or discounts

Gross profit – sales revenue less the costs of goods sold (i.e. the costs incurred in the production of something) Gross profit is sometimes expressed as percentage of sales.

Joint venture – a project undertaken by two ore more persons or entities joining together with a view to profit

Liquid assets – financial assets that can quickly be converted into cash

Net profit – gross profit minus all costs. The net profit is the bottom figure on an accounting balance sheet, hence the expression 'the bottom line'.

Profit and loss account – the summary record of a company's sales revenues and expenses over a period, providing a calculation of profits and losses during that time

Return on investment (ROI) – a ratio of the profit made in a financial year as a percentage of an investment. The higher the percentage figure, the greater the perceived return.

Working capital – the funds and assets readily available to run a business

Bear in mind that there's no such thing as a 'typical' cost — franchises come in all shapes and sizes in a dizzying variety of industry sectors. If you're signing up to become a franchisee, an ethical franchisor will let you know about working capital and other costs involved. Research the prospectus carefully and ask as many questions as you need to for full clarification and understanding. Be wary of people who gloss over questions or dismiss them as unimportant: if they matter to you, they *are* important. Some, or all, of the following elements will need to be considered as you look at investing in franchising, either as franchisee or franchisor:

Investment

- total investment
- working capital
- liquid requirement

Take references from the franchisor's bankers so that you can make sure they are a financially viable operation. Also look at the franchisor's audited accounts and trading figures — you need to know how much capital is invested in the business and how profitable it is.

Initial fee

- licence to use
- initial training
- set-up and equipment
- launch

Continuing fees

- product and service development
- training and personal development
- consultancy support
- promotions and advertising
- management service fee (MSF)
- staffing costs

Additional considerations for franchisors

- market research
- franchisee recruitment
- legal fees
- operating manual – fees for specialist collation
- pilot test period

Financial preparation for franchisees

If becoming a franchisee is your goal, talk to existing franchisees about the finances and how they work. Take off your rose-tinted glasses and discuss difficulties as well as marvellous sales figures that 'go beyond all expectations'.

Have the right financial team behind you

Having the right financial advice is essential. For example, your choice of accountant will affect your franchise business from day one, so much so that your chances of success can depend on the advice, knowledge and level of service you receive from him or her.

The accountant

Before signing your franchise agreement, you should appoint an accountant who has experience within the franchise industry so that he or she is able to offer you advice on the business formation, any issues with HM Revenue and Customs and, in particular, the franchise contractual requirements for your accounting records. You'll find a list of accountants who are familiar with franchising on the BFA website in the Helpful advice/Professional advisors section.

Here is a checklist of things to find out about prospective accountants.

1 **Do they provide a free initial consultation?** If you can clarify the main issues of business formation, tax, VAT, accounting software and record-keeping at this initial consultation for no cost, it will greatly reduce your set-up expenses.

2 **Are they affiliated members of the British Franchise Association?** If your accountant is an affiliate member of the BFA, you have the assurance he/she understands the concept of franchising, the contractual relationship between franchisor and

franchisee, and the accounting requirements and obligations imposed on the franchisee.

3 **Are they members of a recognised accounting institute or association (Chartered or Certified)?** If your accountant is a member of a recognised accounting institute or association, he or she will work to industry standards, giving you added peace of mind. Find out about their qualifications and how many partners there are in the practice.

4 **Do they provide business formation advice?** How you set up and form your business (sole trader, partnership or limited company) can have serious implications and an effect on obtaining funding for the business, past and future tax liabilities of the business, and the future structure of the business.

5 **Do they have a dedicated franchise team that has experience in the franchise industry?** How many franchisors do they deal with? Do they have experience of franchising within your chosen franchise business and can their accounts team comply with the accounting requirements as laid down in your franchise agreement?

6 **Can they provide a free helpline for all their services?** Support for your entire accounting and financial requirements can be extremely important and helpful, leaving you with time to concentrate on

growing your business. However such back-up can become expensive, so a *free* helpline is invaluable. Also ask about their estimated response times.

7 **Do they provide additional services such as payroll, bookkeeping, VAT accounting and stock control?** Check the various services offered, as some accountants will prepare annual accounts and provide taxation advice but do not necessarily provide the additional services such as monthly management accounts or stock control. Find out if they offer any additional services – e.g. inheritance planning or advice on information systems.

8 **Can they provide remote online accounting services?** With online accounting services, you can have complete flexibility regarding the amount of processing you carry out and how much your accountant carries out. Transfer of data, back-ups and restoring data are no longer required, and you have the security of offsite daily back-ups.

9 **Are their fees good value and fixed where possible?** Try to obtain fixed quoted fees wherever possible to avoid any unpleasant surprises at the end of the year.

10 **Can they provide the accounting services required by your franchise agreement, e.g. monthly management accounts?** Many franchise agreements now require franchisees to submit

monthly management accounts in an agreed
format to the franchisor.

And last but by no means least, find out who will look after
your business on a day-to-day basis. You want to be sure that
you will work well together. Culture and Credentials!

By completing the above checklist, you stand a good
chance of getting the right advice, at the right time, at a competitive cost and complying with all your accounting, payroll
and taxation requirements.

The bank

Your accountant is just one part of your financial arrangements. You may well need to borrow money and you will
almost certainly be operating a bank account. Not all banks
are familiar with franchising so, as with lawyers and accountants, find a bank who will be 100% supportive in your
business venture. Your own bank may have a specialist franchising unit, so it would make sense to check with them first. If
they don't offer this service, the BFA website has a list of
member banks that you could try instead.

In general, banks like dealing with clients who are in the
franchise business because their business is more likely to be
profitable and less likely to fail. As a franchisee, you are less of
a risk with a tried, tested and proven business model in place.
Banks also like the fact that you have (or should have):

- ongoing support from your franchisor
- training in place
- buying power
- brand recognition

These factors mean that you're more likely to grow your business more quickly than others entering the market on their own. Contrary to popular belief, banks *want* to lend money, and very often you will be offered preferential terms as a franchisee ahead of a normal start-up business.

Banks can also be a good source of support at the planning stage. Most of them have templates you can use for business plans and of course they can help with financial forecasting. They also have a 'big-picture' view and will have experience of dealing with a variety of franchises. It should be a big warning sign to you if a bank won't lend you money for a franchise.

Business plans

A business plan is essential for all businesses, however mature they are. It is a key document when you are seeking funding. Your business plan will help potential investors/lenders to understand your vision and goals for the business, how you are going to spend their money and how this will benefit your business as well as them.

Your business plan isn't just useful for fundraising. There are three main areas where it is beneficial:

> *The franchising marketplace as a whole is generally optimistic about [its] future, although less so about the economy generally. When asked about their expectations over the next 12 months, 82% of franchisors and 56% of franchisees forecast an improvement in their business[4].*

1   It gives your business a sense of direction.
2   It convinces others that you have a sense of direction.
3   It helps build commitment because you have publicly announced your objectives.

It also gives you something to measure your progress against – helping you to identify issues early on and take appropriate action.

There's no standard format for a business plan and you'll need to tailor the emphasis towards your own requirements. I remember one bank manager saying how he groans when a boring looking, 100-page business plan that uses tiny typeface

4 Source: Natwest/BFA survey 2008

arrives. Such documents are likely to end up in the recycling bin, so think of the intended audience when writing your plan.

Your **bank** will be interested in:

- how you intend to repay a loan or overdraft
- what you are going to do with the money
- how the loan will help the business to grow
- what other loan or debt commitments you have

Tell **potential investors** about:

- what you are going to do with the money
- when and how you are going to pay it back
- the expected return
- your other sources of funding
- your (management's) track record

Above all, make sure that your plan is honest and realistic, showing your commitment to the business. You can do this by undertaking to:

- re-invest profits from the business rather than taking dividends yourself
- putting in more of your own cash
- using personal borrowings (e.g. mortgage) and guarantees to raise funds

■ finding funds from family, friends and existing
investors

Remember that money attracts money. The more backers you
have, the easier it is to attract new ones. Detail the backing
you already have in your plan.

However, the plan is not just for investors/lenders. Written
well, it can serve as a working document for you as you
develop your business. The layout will be up to you but must
act as a sales and marketing tool by looking the part and projecting your professionalism. Check the layout with a trusted
team member and, if need be, you do the number-crunching
and detail while someone else designs it.

Some essential elements of a business plan are listed
below:

■ **Executive summary.** This section highlights the
main points that you want to catch the reader's
attention. If you can keep it to one sheet of A4,
that will be ideal. You'll need to include details of
key personnel, with an organisational chart (if you
have one).
■ **Market research.** Show here that you know the
market you are entering. Include details of your
competitors, who your potential customers are
and why you think they'll buy your product or

service. It's important to take a dispassionate look at growth potential and to make sure that if you proceed to a pilot, that pilot will measure the market potential as accurately as possible.

- **Marketing plan.** This section will show how you are going to tell your customers/potential franchisees about your product or service. It will include assumptions you have made when setting your targets, for example seasonality, volume, market price trends and so on.

- **Financial information.** You are likely to need help from your accountant for this element of your business plan; it is certainly the section that requires the finest of toothcombs run over it. Include balance sheets, profit and loss account details, information about how you will manage credit, expenditure, stock planning and control. When seeking funding, you'll also need to include a cash-flow forecast and financial forecasts for a three- to five-year period. If the whole prospect of this fills you with horror, don't panic! Start a month at a time and build a picture that grows to a year. Work through that with your accountant, and he or she will advise you how to extend it to three years, if that's what is required.

Doing a business plan isn't as hard as you might think. You don't have to write a doctoral thesis or a novel. Useful books and software packages can help, as can your local Business Link. There is also a lot of good information available online, and a couple of the best websites are listed at the end of the chapter. Be aware, however, of the 'Top 10 business plan mistakes to avoid', as listed by Alan Gleeson on Bplans.co.uk:

1 incredible financial projections
2 lack of viable opportunity
3 no clear route to market
4 overestimation of revenues
5 lack of appreciation of cash-flow management
6 no clear objective
7 no evidence of real demand
8 business plan inconsistencies
9 playing down the competition
10 rushing the output

To summarise, you need to be completely clear about your financial requirements and the demands that you will be under as a franchisee. Don't part with any money before signing documents unless you are 100% sure about what you are agreeing to.

Key points

- Work with a good accountant who has franchising experience.
- If you're borrowing money, don't be frightened of considering worst-case interest rate scenarios.
- Put regular reality checks in place.
- Review your finances monthly.
- Review your time management.
- Everything is negotiable – except the franchise agreement!

Things to watch out for

- Hidden costs along the way.
- Price increases after initial payments.
- Whether you are free to source your own wholesale product.
- Activities that will take longer than you have planned.
- Companies desperate to lend you more money than you need 'for your peace of mind'.
- Loan agreements that change with the market.

Helpful resources

The Franchise Alliance – **www.franaccounts.co.uk**

The Natwest/BFA survey – to view it, visit **www.natwest.com/**

**business/day-to-day/industry-and-community-services/
g1/franchising/natwest-BFA-survey.ashx**

Business Link Helpline – 0845 600 9 006

Tools and comments on writing a business plan – **www.
bplans.co.uk**

Templates for business and marketing plans – **www.
microsoftoffice.com**

6

UNDERSTANDING THE IMPORTANCE OF THE FRANCHISE AGREEMENT, OPERATIONS MANUAL AND CHECKING CREDENTIALS

This chapter covers three key elements of franchising that are equally important for franchisees and franchisors. Although the franchisor prepares the franchise agreement and operations manual, they are critical tools for the success of the franchise from both perspectives.

The franchise agreement

A game of football runs much more smoothly with a clearly marked pitch, correctly sized goals, a qualified referee and two teams who know and play by the rules. The franchise agreement is the set of rules to play by and makes the game run smoothly. It also acts as the referee, in that it outlines what is expected of participants as well as what they are responsible for. Franchisors will have invested heavily in their brand and must ensure it is protected, so if you're a franchisee, don't be surprised if an agreement is in their favour and, in many cases, inflexible. Overall, though, there should be a sense of 'I win, you win' if business is going to flourish for both parties.

I win	⟷	You lose
You win	⟷	I lose
I win	⟷	You win

Legal advice for franchisees and franchisors

Buying a franchise is different in important ways from buying another business. As a franchisee, you will be entering into a long-term relationship with your franchisor, who you will have to rely on to a large extent for the success of your own business. You will not be allowed to run things as you think fit, but precisely in accordance with your franchisor's system. Franchisors must rely on their franchisees to build a successful part of their network.

Both sides must consider all the risks, which include:

- inadequate pilot testing (by the franchisor)
- poor franchisee selection
- bad structuring of the franchise
- under-capitalisation of the franchisor or franchisee
- poor running of the business by the franchisor
- competitive risks

There are various legal stages that you will have to go through before you buy a franchise.

1 Sign a confidentiality agreement, if confidential information is being provided. A confidentiality agreement is sometimes called an NDC (non-disclosure contract).
2 Enter into a deposit agreement, which will require payment to be made to the franchisor. Do take care as the payment may be non-refundable.
3 Obtain a copy of the franchise agreement.
4 Obtain professional legal advice on the agreement.
5 Obtain legal advice on premises if the franchise is premises-based.
6 Sign the franchise agreement and make the payment as required in the agreement.

The franchise agreement is the legal basis for the relationship, and it's crucial. Don't sign any document, or pay any fees or deposit, until you have taken specialist legal advice from a solicitor. Ask for a specimen contract to review, if it isn't offered to you automatically.

There are three fundamental objectives of a franchise agreement:

1   As there is no specific franchise legislation, it should contractually bind the franchisee and franchisor and accurately reflect the terms agreed upon.
2   It should seek to protect the benefit of both the franchisor and the franchisee, and the franchisor's intellectual property.
3   It should clearly set out the rules by which the game will be played.

Normal contract features include the following:

■   Identification of the franchisor's **proprietary interests**.

- The **nature and extent of the rights granted** to the franchisee.
- **Territory.** What area does the franchise cover? Does the franchisee have exclusive rights to sell within it?
- **Term of the agreement and renewal.** How long does the franchise last? Will the franchisee have the option to renew it, and on what terms? The term must be long enough for the franchisee to recoup his or her investment and make a return from building up the business. Most franchise agreements provide a qualified right of renewal.
- **Fees payable**, initial and ongoing. What initial fee will the franchisee pay? What percentage of sales revenue will the franchisee pay? Will a regular management fee need to be paid – and if so, what does it cover? Will you have to pay other costs? How are the costs worked out? Understand, before it's too late, the financial implications of your agreement.
- The **extent of the services** provided by the franchisor, both initially and on a continuing basis.

How much help will you get starting the business? What continuing support will you get?

- The **initial and continuing obligations of the franchisee.** These range from business set-up as you comply with the franchisor's requirements, to undertakings to comply with operating, accounting and other administrative systems. After training to operate the business successfully, you will be subject to non-compete and confidentiality obligations.

- **Restrictions.** What restrictions are there on what you're allowed to do and how you must run the business?

- Any **operational controls imposed on the franchisee** (such as using stipulated suppliers, or operating in agreed territories). These are intended to ensure that operational standards are properly maintained. The failure to maintain standards by one franchisee can harm the entire network.

- **Sale of the business.** Can you build up the business and sell with a capital gain? There will always be controls. If there aren't any, you should be suspicious! You must be able to see how you could sell the business.

- The **death of the franchisee.** Can the business be preserved as an asset and sold/taken over by your dependants if they can qualify as a franchisee?

- **Exit.** What happens if you can't continue in business for some reason – perhaps due to ill health? What happens if you want to sell your franchise?

- **Termination and consequences.** Any breach of the agreement may lead to its termination – but you should have the opportunity to put right minor remediable breaches. However, if you decide to terminate the agreement yourself, you will lose the use of the trademark/trade name and other rights owned by the franchisor. You will be under an obligation for a reasonable period not to compete with the network, and prohibited from using the franchisor's system and methods. The franchisor may have options to buy the business. Valuation provisions should be carefully checked!

The operations manual (prepared by the franchisor)

If you're wondering why this is in the legal section, it is because the manual has important significance in law. The franchise agreement refers to the manual, and it is essential that the two documents are consistent. Also, in the event of dispute with a franchisee, it is of course very helpful to have the operating system documented. However, despite its practical and legal importance, franchisors rarely pay enough attention to the content of their manual. As you start to prepare it, it will challenge the way you currently operate. Comments such as 'we've always done it that way' will need to be challenged and understood. Can you make improvements? Have you explained the logic behind the most commonsense items? To take a simple example, do you use first or second class postage, Royal Mail Special Delivery or courier? The variance in costs will be considerable across a year of business if you are sending out large volumes of post. Your franchise manual is the A–Z of how to operate. The reader should be able to pick it up, receive your training and then run the business on their own – with access to your support team, obviously.

What should be in a franchise operations manual?

The primary purpose of the franchise manual is to support the operations of the business – in other words, to help the people working in the franchise to do their jobs. A franchise manual should set out the following inter-related aspects of an operating business:

- what the roles within the business are. For example, Dave and Pete may have driven the vans since day one as well as doing a variety of other jobs. Rather than describing the roles as 'Dave's job' and 'Pete's job', though, you need to categorise them in terms of function: driver, printer, cleaner and so on — whatever is appropriate for your business
- what the main processes or activities of the business are
- the tasks that are performed by employees of each role in each area
- the performance standards that attach to the tasks and activities
- what the mechanisms for process management and improvement are
- all issues related to brand identity — everything from stationery to building layout and colour schemes

Who should write it?

The critical nature of this document means you must choose the most competent resource(s) you have at your disposal to compile it. You will have to figure out whether this is you (the business owner), your key employees, or specialists you bring in to do the job. As you'll see on various franchise-related websites, there are several companies who claim independence and the ability to help write your manual. They will charge for their services, though, and you must include that in your financial planning.

It's important too to remember that franchise systems never remain static – in fact franchisors have a duty to enhance their operating systems over time. As these mature, the operating system will develop, the legal agreement may change, the profile and nature of the franchisee business may change and the overall culture of the system may evolve. Therefore, the content of the manual can quickly get outdated. Are you, the business owner, the right person to be keeping it up to date? An independent eye will usually offer excellent value. However, if working with a consultant, you must be sure they have franchising experience. Check their credentials, ask to see examples of their work and talk to their existing clients.

Hard or soft copy?

My suggestion would be to have both. You'll produce a soft (electronic) copy as you prepare the manual – which is easy to amend and can be distributed electronically – but a professionally laid-out hard copy will serve you well and be a simple reference point for franchisees. You can also take a manual with you when seeking finance. The downside with hard copies is that they must be kept up to date, and you have to ensure franchisees act upon your re-issues. Working through a hard-copy manual at a training session brings it to life. With all the effort that is going to go into preparing the operations manual, you can see now why you must protect your intellectual property, trademark, and so on.

When should the manual be written?

The manual will outline the many complex activities that go into running your franchise business, so it should be written *before* you have any franchisees. The process of writing it will give you the opportunity to visualise absolutely everything that is required, as well as highlighting areas that must be addressed as part of your preparation for franchising your business. When looking for funding, this document will show that you are taking franchising seriously, as well as the fact that you know what you're doing.

The phases of writing

The process of writing a franchise manual is similar to that of writing any technical, reference or training document aimed at an end-user who needs to be supported to do particular things. It needs to communicate very clearly and precisely, and you should work through the following phases as you write:

- Defining the purpose of the document – this will open your eyes about how you currently operate and possibly challenge you to review some of your practices.
- Analysing audiences, tasks and information needs – each individual task needs to be defined in terms of characteristics and responsibilities. You may find it helpful to complete an individual job specification for each task. This may seem over the top for a small business, but this is key to transferring the business elsewhere. Note that tasks need to be separated from people. A new franchise will start with no people!
- Determining the contents – build a framework of key headline topics to be covered.
- Writing the contents – don't underestimate how long this will take. Get help!
- Reviewing and evaluating, fine tuning, and publishing/printing – the first three will happen many times before the manual is ready to publish. You may find gaps or duplications in the business not otherwise spotted. Now is your opportunity to present the manual to your trusted team to read as if they were new franchisees. Do they understand it all? How can it be improved? Don't do this part in a

rush. Once you have what you consider to be the final version, sleep on it. Leave it for 24–48 hours to clear your mind and then take a fresh look. Spelling errors have a habit of hiding until you see the hard copy!

Checking credentials

Checking credentials is part of 'due diligence', the process you go through to establish the viability of the franchise you wish to buy or set up. In short, franchisors want to be sure their franchisees will add value to their growing business. And franchisees want to invest in and commit to a secure business model. When making a large purchase such as buying a house, we look carefully at its credentials: is a motorway about to be built through the front garden; how long will the lease last; are the electrics up to standard and so on. We know we like the house, its aspect and the possibilities for making it our own, but we have to go through the other information to save time, money and disappointment at a later stage.

The same is true of starting in the franchise business, in respect of checking credentials. The excitement of a new project with all its possibilities of fresh success could easily suppress the wise cynic in you. But this part of setting up a franchise is about going in with your eyes wide open and is as important for a potential franchisee as it is for a franchisor.

Checking potential franchisors' credentials

One of the UK[5] banks lists the following warning signs to be on the lookout for – they could be indicators of a potentially bad franchisor:

- large, unjustified up-front fees
- not much emphasis on training/support
- negotiable agreements – for example, 'sign today for a discounted price; sign next week and it'll cost you an additional amount'
- no real interest in you and how much you have incestigated them or want to do so
- pushing you to close and sign an agreement based on territory availability
- no proper pilot test for the franchise
- lack of transparency regarding training – for example, stating that anything above basic training will be charged in addition, but with no outline of what you can expect this to be

Delving into the financial stability of a franchise is work for an expert, and you must make the most of your accountant or bank.

5 Lloyds TSB, 'How to franchise your business'

What you need to find out from the franchisor, in addition to items mentioned in Chapter 3

- *The company's financial health and history.* Unless you are happy to take on a high-risk investment, any unfortunate patterns should put you off.

- *How long has the franchise been operating?* Cheaper franchises have often not been operating very long and are at the beginning of their business growth. Unless there are extremely robust pilot results, tread carefully with your investment.

- *Details of pilot operation results.* This is the place where you can see how robust the business model is, as well as how transferable. Watch out for a 'dream ticket' pilot that ran perfectly – did it really run that smoothly, with no need for any changes?

- *Current number of franchisees.* This will give you an idea of how well the model is translating. If you ask about projected growth at the same time, you'll also find out how committed the franchisor is to genuine expansion. It may also set off territorial alarm bells – you could be signing up to an area at an early stage of the franchise, only to see four or five others moving into your patch and diminishing your opportunity to grow.

- *Main source of company earnings.* This is an interesting one to learn about. The franchisor will have a core business that produces the profit. So is franchising just an add-on that could be sidelined at a later date, having secured your investment? This is a cynical thought but one not to be overlooked. Members of the BFA will have sustainable franchise businesses, but there's still no harm in checking.

- *Total cost of taking up the franchise.* No matter how often you have seen this detail written in draft documents or the prospectus, ask for clarification. Don't sign up to anything until you are absolutely sure what you'll be in for.

- *Realistic working capital needed.* The key word here is realistic. Delve down into what will be needed. Find out the average from other franchisees. You don't want to run out of money four months into the new venture.

- *Bank references and other referees.* A bona fide operation will be happy to supply references to you. Your bank is likely to have access to information relating to the franchise you are investigating.

- *Types and amounts of advertising.* This should be clearly laid out in your agreement and the operating manual, but is often an area of consternation and confusion. If you are being asked to commit a percentage of your fee to advertising, be sure you understand the sort of return on investment you can expect. Will your contact details be included on any local advertising? Can you supplement franchisor advertising with your own? National organisations tend to have a pretty good handle on advertising and often employ an advertising agency. Smaller, new franchises could still be testing the water and, without putting too fine a point on it, you could be in danger of flushing good money after bad.

■ *Any need to buy products from the franchisor.* In years one and two of operating, you may be only too pleased to use franchisor suppliers. However, once you understand the business more, you may learn that there are better deals to be had elsewhere. In fact, there nearly always will be, but you need to think about the overall value and time-saving that using a franchisor supplier offers. Find out how the franchisor keeps their rates competitive, so that you can reassure yourself it isn't just due to some cosy supplier arrangement that keeps franchisor profits up at your expense. A legitimate franchisor will be happy to answer your questions.

■ *Target obligations.* In committing to a franchise you must understand the target obligations that will be placed upon you. Look at the pilot or ask other franchisees to see how realistic the targets are. Unreasonable targets that you struggle to meet can affect your cash flow. Remember that you are running your own business and will need to find your own clients. You can't sit back and wait for them to walk through your door with their money.

■ *Realistic profit and loss figures*. Ask your accountant to look at these and, if you are unsure what they mean, explain the implications for your business. If you are borrowing money for this venture, the P&L figures will be particularly relevant as you need to know when you can break even.

■ *Operating restrictions*. These will help you to establish how much you will be able to grow the business in your area and will relate to a variety of issues, including those linked to territory and suppliers. This should be clearly covered in the agreement.

■ *Launch assistance*. This will be vital in a new area. The franchisor should have a good record of what works well and help you to apply it to your franchise. If you have a great track record in PR you will want to be sure you can maximise that experience.

A note about management service fees (MSFs)

If you are a franchisee, the BFA doesn't recommend flat-fee MSFs as the best option, as they mean that the franchisor doesn't have a financial stake in your business. It follows that this could lead to less support and less incentive for them to develop the business. If franchisors are members of the BFA, their financial systems will be vetted to ensure they are robust. Whatever the fee, be sure to understand exactly what it covers and the benefits you are receiving. For example, a fee of 25% of turnover may sound a lot, but if you receive all your accountancy and legal costs within that and they can be valued at 30%, then 25% is fine.

Checking potential franchisees' credentials

You can expect to have to find 40–50 applicants for your franchise in order to find the one you want. The following three points illustrate just how important the checking of credentials will be to you as you set up your franchise:

- 'Franchising is a partnership. A franchise's major asset, once established, is its franchisees.'
- 'A model franchise company will recruit as franchisees people who are not only qualified financially but also by ability, energy and enthusiasm to make the most of the opportunity available to them.'
- 'Setting up a franchise is less difficult than managing it later on – you have to live with your earlier mistakes, and a lot of those are people you pick when the urge for rapid growth takes over from all other considerations.'

When interviewing prospective franchisees, you need to prioritise the qualities you are looking for. Take time to think about your business and the important characteristics and skills required, and tailor your questions accordingly. The word 'credentials' implies that you need to check the financial and management experience of the prospective franchisee as well as their desire to succeed in business. You will, of course, move around in a conversation, but the basic principles of the type of winning franchisee you are looking for are your priority. How you phrase your questions will depend on your own style, but you need to leave as much space as possible for an honest response. Remember, you are trying to get into the head of your potential franchisee to be sure they will work well with you and for the business as a whole. Consider asking questions such as:

- How will you cope with the isolation of self-employment?
- What's your self-discipline like?
- How can you demonstrate your financial viability?
- What's your vision for the growth of this franchise territory?
- Talk about your sales experience.
- This is quite a big step for you. What do your family and friends make of it?
- How can you demonstrate that you are sales-orientated?
- How do you deal with uncertainty?
- What levels of profit are you looking for in the business?
- What steps do you currently take for your personal development and training? (The answer to this should reveal how likely a person is to be open to your training and advice.)
- What's the best way to delegate?
- Why can failures be important to a business?
- What motivates you?

There are a wide variety of personality indicator tools on the market but unless you are qualified in using and interpreting them, beware: it's easy to draw the wrong conclusions. If you really want to use one of these models, think about investing in a consultant to assist you. This is a good route to go down if you have a track record of making poor appointments or you are in completely unfamiliar territory.

Whichever selection method you use, you must secure business references that support potential franchisee statements. Look for specific sales experience that shows results. My preference is actually to speak to referees, either on the phone or in person, as you can often hear things that won't appear on paper (long silences or hesitation, say, which could indicate difficulty in answering a question).

Key points
- Find a good franchise lawyer.
- Understand the language being used.
- Do your due diligence carefully.
- A good agreement will be the basis for building a sustainable business.
- Try before you buy.
- Ask the same questions of each person.
- Ask about difficulties.
- Be systematic and objective, making the most of what you've learned from your pilot.

Things to watch out for
- Beware of complicated systems of payment/ commission that aren't easy to run or manage.

- Learn to read between the lines of what is written and spoken.
- If something unexpected or unwanted appears, delve further.

Helpful resources

The Law Society – **www.lawsociety.co.uk**

Business Link – **www.businesslink.gov.uk**

Manual Writers International – this is a full-service independent publishing consultancy which specialises in producing operational manuals in accordance with your franchise agreement: **www.manual-writers.com**

Howarth Franchising – this organisation can assist with manual writing in accordance with BFA standards; **www.howarthfranchising.com**

Exhibition stand advice and prices – **www.rocksolidpromotions.co.uk**

7 RUNNING YOUR FRANCHISE BUSINESS – THE FIRST YEAR

'TO ME, BUSINESS ISN'T ABOUT WEARING SUITS OR PLEASING STOCKHOLDERS. IT'S ABOUT BEING TRUE TO YOURSELF, YOUR IDEAS AND FOCUSING ON THE ESSENTIALS.'

Richard Branson

Most businesses have a life cycle, as illustrated by the diagram below. The trick is to keep youthful enthusiasm running for the entire life of the business and not to allow cynicism to set in. The franchise business is no exception, and the challenge for franchisor and franchisee alike is to keep the positive momentum going continuously. Innovation, product and personal development, brand growth, accountability and strong working relationships will all contribute to this feeling of vibrancy and energy. A positive attitude is vital too.

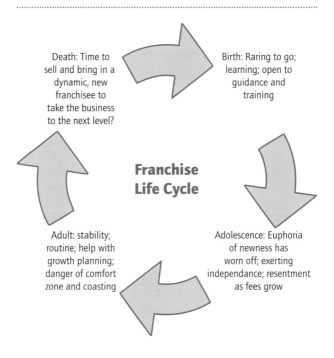

Birth: Raring to go; learning; open to guidance and training

Adolescence: Euphoria of newness has worn off; exerting independance; resentment as fees grow

Adult: stability; routine; help with growth planning; danger of comfort zone and coasting

Death: Time to sell and bring in a dynamic, new franchisee to take the business to the next level?

Franchise Life Cycle

If you're not used to running your own business, there are some simple steps you can take to get you off to a good start. First and foremost, take heed of your franchisor's advice; they will have a heritage of success for a reason. Your franchisor will want you to do well in your business, and the best way to do that is from a firm footing on the day you open your doors to customers. Your confidence will give confidence to those around you, from team members to customers and suppliers. Become a life-long learner who is open to new ideas as well as sharpening your existing business tools. The franchisor will be able to help you with your areas of weakness if you can, employ people whose strengths cover your weaker areas. Spend time strengthening your strengths!

Share best practice

Other franchisees are likely to be a real source of support and inspiration. Much of the advertising and commentary for the franchise industry focuses on the fact that as a franchisee, you are joining a family. Those family members will, more often than not, be keen to support you. Real entrepreneurs will see your success as their success: you're building a brand together and strong franchisees are the best way to do this. If a number of small franchises work well in concert, you can all 'punch above your weight'. Some prefer the expression 1+1=3. Whichever works for you, make the most of franchisor events, awards ceremonies, training sessions etc. that bring franchisees together. Use your networking skills to keep in touch what is happening in other franchise areas. You'll be amazed how simple ideas are transferable to your own business and can make all the difference. Ask questions and keep asking questions – and don't be embarrassed if they seem obvious ones. Find out what makes the successful franchisees successful. Decide which elements you can use in your own operation. As well as learning from others, be prepared to acknowledge what you are doing well – and do more of it! Share ideas with others. You may have a technique that will bring success to another franchisee. Remember, they aren't the competition: you're all in it together.

In addition to communicating with your fellow franchisees, use your local networking events to learn and share best practice. Keep a close eye on what the competition is up to so that you can maintain your competitive edge. Tune in to what's happening in the market and what the forecasts are. If you have concerns about what you hear, talk this through with your trusted advisors and feed back your findings to the franchisor – there may be a national picture emerging. But responding to every market glitch or piece of unsubstantiated gossip will drive you mad and your business into the ground, so try to remain focused solely on what is good for your business.

Remind yourself of your long-term goals

In your first year of franchising, it will be easy to become caught up with the detail and intricacies of the day-to-day running of the business – a common issue for many business people. I call it living with a magnifying glass in your hand: you're bent over a desk studying the minutiae so hard you don't see what's coming at you on the horizon, focusing so much on existing customers you forget to start looking for new ones. The euphoria of your new venture could be carrying you along on a cloud, with minor difficulties overlooked as 'par for the course'. But actually this is the time to be using a strong pair of binoculars on your business. Take them out at least monthly to have a look at the view, the horizon, the market and your business numbers, and get some perspective on how your business is running. Remind yourself about the softer side of your new franchise business. Is it living up to your expectations? How is your family coping with the change? What is working better than expected? What's surprised you? What needs adjusting?

Measure your success along the way

If you don't know where you're going, how will you know when you get there? Think of it as having a map and preparing for a journey. You are now firmly in the driving seat with a franchise business to run and financial commitments to meet. You need to have some way of measuring your success. The best means of doing this is to a have manageable summary page – one side of A4 – with criteria that you can use to assess progress. The franchisor may well be prepared to help you with this as it's in their interest for you to succeed. These measurements can develop into amazing forecasting and projecting tools with month-on-month/year-on-year comparisons. The important thing is to develop a format that means something to you and points your business in a particular direction. For example, start to look at the relationships between measurements. If you're under-staffed, is that creating customer complaints? Are you having enough time away from work to keep fresh? There are some suggestions below for items to include on your list of criteria:

Specific item to review	Target position	Actual position	Difference	Comment
Fees to franchisor	£10,000	£7,000	−£3,000	Ask for franchisor advice
Contract customers	200	180	−20	Weeded out unprofitable biz
New customers	20	40	+20	All projected to be profitable
Gross sales	£20,000	£21,000	+£1,000	
Complaints	<5%	8%	−3%	Related to staff shortage?
Work/life balance	Two school runs per week			Not done a school run yet. Holiday booked for June
Staffing levels	95%	75%	−20%	Related to complaints?
Travel expenses	£2,000	£2,500	−£500	Petrol price increases

A franchisee will be measured by the items in the franchise agreement, so make sure you include all of these in your table.

Managing your franchisees

Franchising your business isn't about selling franchises and then forgetting about them. You have a continuing relationship with your franchisees.

As part of this, you must provide the support detailed in the franchise agreement. This can include:

- helping people to set up their franchise initially
- providing training in how to run the business
- running national promotional campaigns to increase sales
- helping them manage their business effectively
- innovating to keep your product or service ahead of the competition

Doing all this isn't just a matter of fulfilling your contractual obligations. By supporting franchisees, you help them succeed – and increase the fees you receive.

Although it isn't included in the agreement, you also have a role to play in motivating franchisees. New franchisees can find the early months difficult and may become discouraged. Alternatively, successful ones may become complacent and stop trying so hard to increase sales. Again, by motivating them you help yourself.

At the same time, you need to ensure that they are running their businesses the way they should. One of the keys to building a successful brand is consistency. If different franchisees run their businesses differently, your brand can suffer. Your operations manual should give clear information on the correct procedures.

Last but not least, you need efficient administration to ensure that you collect the right franchise fees.

Work SMART

SMART is a favourite business method – the acronym stands for Specific, Measurable, Achievable, Realistic and Time-bound – even if some people shy away from it, thinking that it's used simply as a stick to beat others with. But used carefully and consistently, it can help to create a positive approach to your business, whether you're a franchisor or franchisee. Here's how the components break down.

Specific

This means clearly defined or identified. You should be able to say in one or two sentences precisely what it is you are going towards, as a business. This may sound really basic, but when looking at long-term plans it's easy to paint a big picture and lovely visions that, unless they are specific, will not materialise. Think about the areas of the business you must review regularly for the table, above. Don't work on this alone: involve your trusted team of advisors.

Measurable

The dictionary tells us that something is measurable when you can ascertain the size, amount or degree of it. And that's exactly what you will do with your criteria for reviewing progress of the business. Take each of your specific items to review and think about the best way to measure it. Ask questions such as:

- When will I do it by?
- What is the deadline?
- How much money is that?
- How near to the annual target will that take me?
- How many . . . ?

Achievable

Can whatever you are assessing actually be done? This question applies regardless of the activity, from living up to the corporate vision to leading a team in a certain direction.

- Brainstorm – give all ideas the green light!
- Next, review and analyse ideas – some will get the red light.
- Who needs to be involved in agreeing the goal or vision?

- Start thinking about matching skills to tasks.
- How's your delegation?

Realistic

Being realistic is normally only considered relevant for purely practical tasks (e.g. 'I want to extend our restaurant from 40 to 1,000 covers tomorrow'). However, if what you take back to your business is to be workable, it'll also need to be realistic.

- Beware of taking your red light thinking too far.
- With whom will you do your reality check?
- Now's the time to find an accountability partner whom you trust.

Time-bound

As you set timescales for achieving your vision and goals, think about them in terms of hours, days, months or years. You may well have a three-year goal, but can you set markers at regular intervals along the way? Be honest with yourself and don't set ridiculously short deadlines, but remember that it's equally dangerous to have a never-ending plan that loses momentum.

Think about the following points:

- Setting time boundaries is about creating momentum as well as achieving goals.

- Review your time and priority management. Which of the following would you use to describe your time management: a) excellent, b) good, c) not bad, d) could be better, e) others want me to improve!
- With whom do you need to agree your timelines?
- Who sets your deadlines?
- How manageable are they?
- Think about the need for effective delegation.

Review progress with your trusted team

The trusted team who worked with you on finding your ideal franchise opportunity can help you to keep on track. This is a time where your own personal development is critical, as is the need to 'see the wood for the trees'. Book a meeting for a review of the business's progress and at the same time check how well you, the owner, are doing. Finding a method of receiving and giving positive feedback will be important if you are to make the most of the meetings and not waste your time and the team's in chatting.

Keep close to the numbers

With salaries to pay and bank loans/investments to be serviced, keeping a close eye on the finances of your business must become a regular routine for you. These will be one of the indicators that all is going well, or warning signs if not.

Decide, with your accountant or franchisor, which are the key numbers to keep a close eye on. Write them down, update them and ensure that checking them becomes second nature to you.

Make your marketing effort count

The first year is a great time to launch yourself into your local market and become an 'expert' in your area. If you're confident speaking in public, make the most of one-minute 'slots' at networking events. Collect testimonials from contented customers and ask for their permission to use them as part of your marketing efforts. Write articles for local press and trade magazines. When you run a small business, you are your own PR machine. Above all, collect data about your marketing effort – what's worked, what hasn't. What sort of return on investment are you achieving? Measure it!

Learn to delegate

This franchise business may be the first time you have run a team of people, which can be pretty scary at the best of times. If the franchisor offers any management training, sign up for it. If they don't offer training, find some elsewhere.

The simple tool below (© Clifton Consulting) has, over the years, proved effective for the managers and teams I've trained.

Starting at 12 o'clock, read the definitions clockwise. Once you understand these, you can work your way around the clock in a variety of situations, moving in either direction. Although some may seem repetitive, they act as reinforcement and offer the opportunity of confirming and agreeing expectations. You will come to see that this model is helpful for general communication, not just delegation. When you see the word 'delegation' written, think communication. How are you communicating? This model is a great way of avoiding misunderstandings, and an explanation of the definitions follows:

Receiver must see it as a step forward – Whatever you are delegating, you need to show the person to whom you are delegating how the action fits into the big picture: it's important that they don't feel as if they've simply been 'lumbered' with something, but rather that the task could be a personal step forward for them and/or the business.

Know results expected – Be clear about what you are expecting, particularly in terms of timing and deadlines – e.g. report for board meeting required by next Wednesday, format explained, number of copies required etc.

Know the skills and abilities of the team – Finding a round peg for a round hole is the way to go with delegation, which means using the strengths of the team around you. By all means delegate to people who are building their skills base, but be aware that they will need more training and hand-holding along the way.

Performance standards are known – If you're asking someone to provide you with information, explain specifically what you want – for example, a report on an Excel spreadsheet with the specified template and typeface and no calculation errors.

Positive control system is fair – To some people this sounds harsh and smacks of control freak tendencies. However, if you consider that delegating is about letting go, this is the system that allows the letting-go to be measured. This will assist the receiver as well as the delegator to proceed with confidence. A fair control system should be agreed by both parties. So, today is Thursday and the report is needed for the board meeting next Wednesday. A positive control system would set a deadline for the first draft on say, Friday. Then on Tuesday morning, the almost complete report would be reviewed and any changes made. There would be a final run-through on Tuesday afternoon, so that all would be ready for the board meeting the following day.

Sufficient authority allowed – This speaks for itself. Confidential material for a board report may not be accessible to all staff and information may need to be sought from other departments. So the delegator needs to prepare the way for the person they are delegating to – e.g. 'David will be coming to you for your figures. Please can you ensure he has them by Friday close of play.' This is particularly important when a more junior staff member has to approach a senior team member.

Rules must be clear – At this stage on the wheel, you will be clarifying the parameters of the task at hand, including confirmation of the expected results, deadlines and performance standards.

Help is available – When learning to delegate, be aware that you are not abdicating responsibility and leaving a person to sink or swim. It is in your interest to ensure the job is completed correctly and to your standards. Let the person know when you are available to help (but not do the job).

Aspects of delegation

Taking the information above, you can see how working your way around the wheel will allow you to use the delegation process with confidence. Each person has the opportunity to listen, learn and ask questions. More often than not, team members rise to the occasion when being delegated work, and they also feel more valued.

Recognise what works in management

If you're managing a team, no matter how small, be aware of some of the key reasons why managers succeed or fail. Have a look at the two lists below and take an honest, critical look at your management style. Where do you need to make adjustments? What training can you receive to improve your management skills?

The reasons managers fail

- unable or unwilling to organise detail
- set a task he/she is unwilling to do (or try)
- don't pass on company directives/policy with 100% commitment
- view *knowing* as being more important than *doing*
- fear competition from others
- lack creativity and big-picture thinking
- hog the limelight
- are disloyal to staff or company

- abuse power
- don't listen enough
- are so creative that loses sight of reality
- won't delegate
- have favourites
- are inconsistent

Reasons managers succeed

- self-motivation
- are prepared to try new ideas
- are fair, with no favourites or cliques
- stick to a decision
- accept when he/she is wrong and reviews/alters course
- take 100% responsibility for the team
- are great at delegation
- are well organised, with a plan
- give/ask for deadlines and sticks to them
- have confidence that builds confidence in others
- understand the need for detail (but not doing it all)
- set a high personal standard and work ethic

Celebrate before moving on to year two

Don't let your first year of business pass without a celebration of your success, however modest. Your financial measurements will tell you what you have achieved, and if you're still in business, that's a success in itself. Your celebrations don't need to be extravagant or expensive, simply a recognition of what you have achieved as an individual and as a team. It's important to set corporate goals, know when you get there and celebrate, before moving on. Celebrating enables you to catch your breath before working out what's gone well and what you will want to do more of in the second year.

Plan year two

As a franchisee, you will now be used to the system you are operating and can look at areas to sharpen up. Talk through your success with the franchisor and your trusted team. Dust off your business plan; review it to see what needs to change for your second year of trading. Find out if there is any more training you can receive to take you into your second year. Tee up your team for your second year of trading – show them the big-picture vision you have for the business and where they fit into that picture.

Franchisors will need their wits about them as they approach year two. Franchisees have developed their businesses and will be growing in confidence. They need to be stretched in the second year in order to keep going. Look at your development plan to see what new products or ideas you are going to bring to the business. Check out the competition, ensuring your strategies will keep you ahead of them. Have a plan to keep your franchisees motivated.

Whilst nurturing your new franchisees, you must keep your eyes on the horizon and future developments. Look at the life-cycle of a business on page 135: how can you keep the adult stage alive but with the enthusiasm of adolescence?

Key points
- Keep sight of your vision (binoculars).
- Measure your success/progress monthly.
- Employ the right people with the right skill sets.

Things to watch out for
- Focusing on what you do well and ignoring other important elements.
- Assuming you know more than the franchisor.
- Losing sight of your priorities.

Helpful resources
Business balls – this organisation has many business tools to work with, mostly free of charge, and it has a great reference site; see **www.businessballs.com**

Chartered Institute of Personnel & Development – **www.cipd.co.uk**

Business coaching and training models – **www.clifton consulting.com**

8
WHAT TO DO IF THINGS GO WRONG

'THE BEST-LAID PLANS OF MICE AND MEN OFTEN GO AWRY'

From a line in 'To a mouse' by Robert Burns

No matter how carefully a project is planned, something may still go wrong with it. Here is one of the stories I collected when researching for this book. Albeit anonymous here, I know the man concerned and take heart from the fact that he has learned from his experience and is now running another successful business.'

'A friend of mine was running a really successful business as a franchisee. It was an area of business that interested me, so I signed up too. There was a franchise agreement and some excellent training that was all included in the fee of around £9,000 + VAT. The support was working well and the franchisor did all the administration and finance. I'd recovered my initial payment in the first 18 months of business. The way the business worked was that I signed up customers, took payment in the name of the franchisor and then did the work. The franchisor, having cleared the cheque, sent me my 70% of the value. It was a simple system that worked well.

'One day, I noticed that payments to me were being delayed. I took no action, assuming it was a delay in the post or the bank clearing system being slow. Next, some of the smaller cheques started to be returned. It took about two weeks to find out that the cheques are returned with advice from the bank. On phoning the franchisor, cheques were re-issued, but they too bounced. Then the bigger cheques started being returned.

'Independently of all this and with no knowledge of what was going on, a customer of mine mentioned to me that there were County Court judgements against the franchisor. When I checked, the franchisor reassured me that it was an administrative error relating to VAT. I believed him.

'Shortly after that, I had a phone call to say the franchisor had gone into voluntary liquidation. My business went with it and there was no opportunity for me to recoup any of my losses. Subsequently I discovered that the franchisor directors had siphoned thousands of pounds from the business.

'What have I learned from this experience? Well, I'd be much more rigorous with my due diligence and include a check on the directors' credentials. You can do that easily through your accountant. The other thing I'd do is to use a solicitor who has experience with franchising.'

Despite your best-laid plans and preparation, things can still go wrong, often because of issues over which you have no control. Perhaps a franchisee isn't delivering their promised financial return to you on time, or a franchisor has become over-stretched and either goes out of business or wants to change previously agreed parameters.

If this happens, your first step — whether you're a franchisor or franchisee — is to collect the facts together in as simple a format as possible. This will enable you to see the full picture and help you to start understanding what has gone wrong and why. Then congratulate yourself on facing up to the truth of the situation! Many people don't get this far early enough, and a small problem quickly escalates out of control. For example, not having a good system for collecting payments may be just about acceptable for one month, but six months later your business could close as a result of not having simple systems in place.

Have you selected the wrong type of person to be a franchisee?

As a franchisor, you will have systems in place to monitor new franchisee businesses as well as to help them develop. While due diligence will help you find out certain things, there may still be gaps you can't spot until the franchise is underway. (This cuts both ways, though: as the case history above tells us, franchisees need to do their due diligence on potential franchisors thoroughly.)

Take note of warning signs and take action early, bringing your concerns to the franchisee clearly and specifically. If it's a relatively minor matter or one where training might be useful, offer help. Ask questions to find out what lies behind the problem. Remember, a weak franchise will undermine your brand and you cannot afford this. Customers are 12 times more likely to share their bad experiences with friends than they are to extol the virtues of a particular company, so bear this in mind when you learn that you have a weak franchisee in your midst and nip problems in the bud as they arise. Your franchise agreement must include specific performance standards and requirements – now is the time to bring them to the fore and ensure the franchisee is complying.

Conflict is healthy!

Few people actively welcome conflict, but running away from an issue won't help. More often than not, a good, open conversation can clarify a situation and bring about simple resolutions. Look at the arrow below, noting how near conflict lies to the most productive end of the arrow. This diagram shows how people respond to change, of which there is likely to be plenty as franchisee operates a new system and franchisor has new franchisee to manage. Conflict is only two steps away from the place where you are making things happen.

Response to change

Most productive

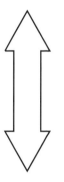

Least productive

Making things happen
Planing
Problem-solving
Confronting
Moaning and groaning
Blaming
Avoiding
Denial
Passive resistance
Active resistance
Sabotage

Why things go wrong

Business specialists have recorded five key reasons why a franchise may fail[1]. These are not generic business problems but specifically related to franchises:

1 LloydsTSB, "How to franchise your business"

1   Business fraud – for example, using celebrities to attract franchisees to systems that were not well-founded, as happened in the USA during the 1960s and 1970s.

2   Intrasystem competition – which occurs when outlets are located too closely together, or company-owned outlets are too near franchised outlets. The result is that each outlet cannibalises the other's sales, although the franchisor may only see this as a way of earning the maximum level of MSF income, ignoring the long-term effects on the system.

3   Insufficient support – if too little is invested in supporting franchises – with pre-launch programmes, management assistance, advertising etc. – the outlets may simply wither away.

4   Poor franchisee screening – this can bring a mismatch between the criteria required for success and the qualities of franchisees actually recruited. Sometimes this arises because a franchisor wants to maximise his or her initial fee income.

5   Persistent conflict between franchisor and franchisee – faults can arise on either side and for a variety of reasons. This is not a positive place to operate a business and can lead to failure.

When communication fails between the franchisee and franchisor

There can be a variety of reasons for a communication failure. Possible solutions will be more likely if a recognised third party can assist. Members of the BFA have signed up to a particular code of conduct and ethics, so that's a natural place to begin. Even though the BFA has neither the power nor the right to intervene in a dispute between franchisor and franchisee, it can nonetheless make a positive contribution in terms of dispute resolution by supporting the re-establishment of positive communication between the parties.

In most cases, complaints by a franchisor against a franchisee are handled directly via the process set out in the franchise agreement. When franchisees have complaints against franchisors, however, the BFA can be used as a catalyst for discussion. In the first instance, the BFA seeks to facilitate an informal conciliation by allowing each party to represent their case and reconsider their positions in order to work towards agreement. The franchisee is invited to complete and return a Notification of Dispute form. Assuming he or she has already pursued all reasonable avenues to resolve the dispute, the BFA will then seek a response from its member franchisor. Often this is sufficient to re-establish constructive dialogue.

The BFA will not make any comment or judgement regarding either party's actions. It does, however, reserve the right to act independently (in total confidence) to address issues of underlying ethical principles with its member franchisors.

Mediation

If an informal conciliation process does not work, the BFA has an independent mediation service which is open to both parties, to allow an amicable resolution of disputes. This is a completely voluntary process which involves independent, qualified mediators with recognised expertise in the franchise sector.

Mediation is a process of structured negotiation between the parties. The mediator is an independent third party who tries to help and facilitate negotiations between the parties. The negotiations will be on a without-prejudice basis, and the two sides are not bound to settle their dispute. The mediator does not give an award (i.e. a judgement) or make a decision, but any settlement reached by the parties will be recorded in writing and will be final and binding. The settlement can be enforced, although not in the same way as an arbitrator's award (see below). The parties can walk away from the mediation at any stage.

Mediation is intended to be a quicker and cheaper option than arbitration (or litigation). It can be used prior to or at any stage during arbitration or litigation. The following is an extract from what a member wrote following use of the BFA's mediation scheme. *'A belated e-mail to let you know that this issue was settled at mediation on Tuesday. XXX did an excellent job for us and I believe we reached a fair outcome . . . we spent £12k in legal fees over 14 months, when the mediation cost us about £1600 all in and was done in less than a day! Thanks for facilitating.'*

However you choose to resolve communication issues, it is recommended that you seek independent legal advice from an experienced franchise lawyer. You can find out more about the rules of mediation on the BFA website.

Arbitration

This is very similar in many respects to litigation. The parties to a dispute will have an arbitrator (an individual like a judge) to decide the issues between them. The arbitrator will conduct the arbitration in accordance with the BFA'S Arbitration Scheme's rules and the provisions of the Arbitration Act 1996.

Arbitration is quite formal in terms of the procedure followed and the manner in which it is conducted, and therefore is very much like litigation. The arbitrator will make an award (a decision or judgement) that is final and binding on the parties (there are or may be limited rights of appeal) and this award is enforceable. The arbitrator will charge fees for undertaking the arbitration, and costs can be awarded against the parties as determined by the arbitrator. Should you use the BFA to assist with your arbitration, it will offer independent arbitrators and you can read the rules on its website.

Key points

- Take your head out of the sand as early as possible!
- Be up-front with business partners/supporters about the situation.
- Be specific about what has gone wrong.
- Understand what has gone wrong and how you can fix it long-term.

Things to watch out for

- Not reviewing your business regularly enough to spot problems on the horizon.
- Thinking you're the only person with this problem.

Helpful resources

- Your lawyer, accountant and/or bank
- Details of the BFA's Mediation Scheme are available at www.thebfs.org/arbscheme/mediationscheme.asp

9 NON-TRADITIONAL FRANCHISE OPTIONS

> There are other types of arrangements that are sales relationships, referred to as franchises. Unless you have a specific franchise agreement that complies with the BFA codes and ethics, however, it is not a franchise.

For example:

- *Distributorship and dealership* – you sell the product but don't usually trade under the franchise name (for example, cars and vans). You have more freedom over how you run the business.
- *Agency* – you sell goods or services on behalf of the supplier. Even though this isn't a classic franchise (where you are buying a system), you

must ensure whatever you have agreed is in writing. Commissions, use of brand and marketing can all be areas of miscommunication and conflict.

- *Event franchising* – this is the hosting of public events in other geographical areas, whilst retaining the original brand, logo, mission, concept and format of the event. As in classic franchising, event franchising is built on copying successful events precisely. A good example of event franchising is the World Economic Forum.

- *Licensee* – you have a licence giving you the right to make and sell the licensor's product. There are usually no extra restrictions on how you run your business. Nevertheless, cover all your bases and be sure you know what you are permitted and not permitted to do. Consider what percentage of your business will be dependent upon the licence.

- According to Wikipedia, *multi-level marketing (MLM),* also known as *network marketing*, 'is a business distribution model that allows a parent multi-level marketing company to market their products directly to consumers by means of relationship referral and direct selling'.

Distributors sit within a hierarchy, earning a commission based on the sales efforts of their organisation, which includes their independent sales effort as well as the leveraged sales of their downline. Commissions are paid to multi-level marketing distributors according to the company's compensation plan. There can be multiple levels of people receiving royalties from one person's sales.

Criticisms have been raised against MLM programmes for being cult-like in nature. Some MLM programmes feature intense motivational programmes which can be hard to distinguish from cult propaganda. So-called corporate cults are businesses whose techniques to gain associate commitment and loyalty are in some ways similar to those used by traditional cults.

Take care here: some businesses offer franchises that are really multi-level marketing. Self-employed distributors sell goods on a manufacturer's behalf. You get commission on any sales you make and also on sales made by other distributors you recruit. You need to recognise that some multi-level marketing schemes may be dishonest or illegal. If you're signing up to anything, run it past your franchise lawyer.

Pyramid schemes

Pyramid schemes are non-sustainable business models that involve the exchange of money primarily by enrolling other people into the scheme, usually without any product or service being delivered. Pyramid selling has been known to come in many guises and is illegal in in many countries, including the US, the UK, France, Canada, Australia, New Zealand and Japan. These types of schemes have existed for at least a century and are *not* franchises.

Social enterprise franchises

'WE BELIEVE IN SOCIAL ENTERPRISE AND DON'T WANT IT TO BE IN THE DOMAIN OF A SELECT FEW WHO UNDERSTAND IT. EVERYONE CAN HAVE SOCIAL VALUES AND BELIEVE IN, AND BENEFIT FROM, SOCIAL ENTERPRISE.'

The North East Social Enterprise Partnership

A social enterprise is a sustainable business with social good at its core. The Office of the Third Sector (part of the UK Cabinet Office) has recently defined social enterprises (SEs) as:

'businesses with primarily social objectives whose surpluses are principally reinvested for that purpose in the business or community, rather than being driven by the need to maximise profit for shareholders and owners.'

Social enterprises can be financially successful and still be true to their objectives. Financial success (or profit) is not to be disregarded or avoided – social businesses need to be viable too. Even if growth isn't the key objective of the social enterprise, profit (or 'surpluses' as the Office of the Third Sector calls it) can help realise a sustainable business. 'Aiming for social profits not just financial profits' sums this up.

And social enterprise isn't just about business with a conscience; it is hugely more than that. It is about delivering change. It's fascinatingly and sometimes frustratingly tough – because the business still has to be competitive – but it is vital to making the UK a fairer and more inclusive society.

If you're wondering what the difference is between a social enterprise and a charity, it can be difficult to spot. Both share similar or identical social aims and objectives. Both seem to do the same work. Perhaps the simplest difference to identify relates to funding. Many charities rely on grants or donations to continue their work, whereas – increasingly – social enterprises and their numerous social business offspring seek to develop their own income stream to meet their objectives. It's a move away from being reliant upon grants and towards creating wealth or profit to sustain a business in the longer term, in a self-sufficient fashion. An example of the difference would be Shelter and The Big Issue – both aim to help the homeless, but the first is a charity and the second is a social enterprise.

Social enterprises contribute to society in many ways. They:

- tackle social and environmental problems
- set new standards
- raise the bar for corporate responsibility
- improve public services and shape public service design, particularly as ethical consumerism increases in popularity
- offer a high level of engagement with users and a capacity to build their trust
- pioneer new approaches
- attract new people to business
- encourage under-represented groups

Social enterprise franchising doesn't mean buying a 'Subway/ McDonalds/Joe Bloggs' franchise and giving 10% of the profit to charity. But if you understand franchising, cloning (see page 64) and solving a social problem, you're getting there.

Building community

Social franchising means using and developing the franchising method to achieve social goals. It is about spreading experience from successful social enterprises so that more people become employed. And these companies apply democracy in such a way that the potential of all employees is developed. Social franchising also builds a community by stimulating contacts among employees in different companies and combining efforts toward common goals.

In social franchising, there is a founder, just as in any other kind of franchise. The starting point for the franchisor is to spread ideas, share experiences, and build a community. The social goals are fundamental, and often include contributing to the creation of more jobs. In this form of franchising, exchange and learning through contacts with those who started earlier are important for the entrepreneurs.

The founder builds up a franchise system and becomes a franchisor. The forms vary among different systems. They can be cooperatives when this is appropriate, but the franchisor always enters into an agreement with the franchisee that regulates rights and obligations. Through involvement, knowledge and fees, the franchisee contributes to the development of the business concept.

Knowledge transfer

By defining the keys to success, documenting these in manuals and developing training courses based on them, a group of entrepreneurs can gain access to knowledge and experience.

In social franchising, an important aspect is training as a source of support for entrepreneurs. This, along with the forms of management and routines, is designed to empower the employees. As a part of every new franchise's founding, everyone is involved in the design of the organisation.

Starting a social enterprise is usually difficult. Entrepreneurs have often been without a foothold in the labour market, with all the attendant disadvantages that go with such a situation. Knowledge and networks for operating a business may not be the best in all cases. Through franchising, however, more social enterprises will be able to start. It provides a support structure for social enterprises and, by co-operating in a franchise organisation, competitiveness is improved. Joint development and quality efforts offer better prospects, but even the social enterprise must survive rapid changes in its commercial environment, so you'll need to keep on the ball.

Agreements and the franchising system

These need to be handled in the same way as in any other franchise, social enterprise or not. The business plan, pilot, operations manual, recruitment process and training all need to be in place in order to operate a successful social franchise.

Case History: Get Hooked on Fishing

Get Hooked on Fishing (www.ghof.org.uk) is a trust that works with local communities to help create opportunities for young people. It delivers fun and interactive training around the sport of angling. The programme is specially designed, with the help of young people, to give the participants more confidence and to demonstrate that there are alternative pathways and better opportunities available to them.

It was originally delivered through Durham Agency against Crime (DAAC), aimed at juveniles who have been identified by local agencies such as the police, Youth Offending Teams (YOTs) and schools as being at risk of falling into crime. The results of the original scheme were amazing, with evidence of reduced truancy and no participants going on to offend. As a consequence, schemes have been set up in various forms around the country seeking to replicate its success.

The trust provides an umbrella structure for

> regionally based schemes, providing direction and
> guidance, and has developed an internal 'charter mark
> system' to ensure quality of delivery at the same time
> as making certain that the staff and volunteers oper-
> ate to a strict code of conduct. The trust has already
> successfully replicated the model over 10 times all
> over the UK.

Key points

- The word 'franchise' is used freely in many areas of
  business. If you're looking in the non-traditional
  direction, that's fine, but don't call an enterprise a
  franchise unless it is one. Over 70% of franchisors
  are affiliated to the British Franchise Association.
  You can do worse than use that affiliation as a first
  guide to legitimacy.

Things to watch out for

- Being unsure of exactly what you are signing up to
  financially.
- What your independent trusted team and advisors
  say about your proposed venture.

Helpful resources

Department for Business, Enterprise and Regulatory Reform Trading Scheme Guide – **www.berr.gov.uk/consumers/ buying-selling/Trading-Schemes/index.html**

Inspire – **www.inspirenortheast.co.uk**

The North East Social Enterprise Partnership – **www.nesep.co.uk**

10 MARKETING YOUR BUSINESS

> 'DRIVE THY BUSINESS OR IT WILL DRIVE THEE.'
> Benjamin Franklin
> *US author, diplomat, inventor, physicist,*
> *politician & printer (1706 – 1790)*
>
> Whatever type of business you run, to survive and thrive you need to tell the world about your marvellous product or service.

If you're a franchisee, whether or not you are supplied with fantastic sales and marketing tools by the franchisor, it is your responsibility to use marketing as one of the tools to make your business a success.

As a franchisor, you will want to maintain brand integrity by keeping a tight rein on marketing materials. That will mean keeping ahead of the game in terms of new product development as well as how your franchisees sell to customers. If 90% of your franchisees ask for changes to the website to improve their ability to sell and thus keep a competitive edge, you've clearly been neglecting this area and need to review it promptly. The other side of this coin is that you don't want to be in a place where you are operating on the whim of every franchisee. You have a successful business model and that is what people are buying into. By franchising your business you are letting go of your intellectual property – it's a tough old world out there so don't let go of it carelessly. Ensure your agreement is watertight and that franchisees are very clear about what type of marketing you are happy with.

Marketing is, in some quarters, considered a martial art. And it can be! The annual marketing budget of just one of the Unilever brands is $29 million and requires whole teams of people, globally, to manage it. However, you are just starting in the franchise business and need to keep life as simple as possible. You can work up to a million-pound marketing budget later on!

'The key to building your business is to develop strong marketing that brings good sales leads. Running a franchise isn't about order-taking or taking the easy option. You have bought an infrastructure and system, *not* a business that runs itself. You have to build the business yourself. If you don't know much about marketing when you take on a franchise, do a course; it will pay dividends.' *Kevin Bourne, Best of Bromley.*

Below are some definitions of marketing. Have a look at them and decide which is the most appealing to you. The key is to keep it simple!

- Marketing is the identification and profitable satisfaction of customers' needs.
- Marketing is the management process responsible for identifying, anticipating, and satisfying customer requirements profitably.
- Selling more products/services to more people.

When you have a proper marketing strategy, it is important to manage it professionally and clearly. If you're the franchisee, everyone in the team, even if there are only two of you, must travel in the same direction and understand what you are doing as well as where you are going. With a clear business direction you can all pull together. If you're the franchisor, it's vital to build your marketing in such a way that the model can be explained and put into practice easily by franchisees. If they can capture your vision for the business, they will transfer that vision across your network. Marketing affects the whole business as well as customers. If it's done well, everyone will *want* to be associated with your brand.

Marketing is there to support, as well as to drive sales and profit

Of course, your marketing strategy must fit into your business plan, whether you are a franchisee or franchisor. Your business plan can be used to measure both how the business is progressing and the effectiveness of your marketing. Both need to be reviewed regularly – *how* regularly is up to you. Whatever you do, agreed outcomes across the business must be established, communicated and then delivered.

If you're new to marketing and haven't been on your course yet, the following points will help you to clarify what can be a baffling world. There are six main elements that need to be considered as you put together your marketing strategy.

1 **Responsibility** – Ask or remind yourself why marketing plays a leading role in your business. Take responsibility for making it work positively. Abdication of responsibility is a common mistake made in business; learn to delegate (see above) and recognise what being responsible means for you and your business.

2 **Identifying** – This brings the SMART tool (see p. 141) to marketing as you need to be specific when approaching your marketing. Examples of the type of things/people you need to identify are as follows:
   - agreed outcomes across the business
   - specific customer(s) so that you can work out their needs and desires and meet these
   - seasonality
   - the competition
   - market trends

- groups of similar customers or potential customers
  - ⇨ prioritise groups by address or franchise territory
  - ⇨ understand their behaviour
  - ⇨ respond with appropriate marketing strategies

3 **Anticipation** – This is a skill you can develop, especially when you realise the benefit it will give to the business. Anticipation could usefully be described as market intelligence. Some of things you can anticipate are shown below.

- how customers behave and live: trends
- what the competition will be up to
- what's ahead – delays – new roads to follow (see the PESTLE tool on p. 188)
- investment required in the business
- staffing levels
- seasonal activity
- possible obstacles
- new opportunities

4 **Satisfaction** – for the customer. The old expression 'the customer is always right' isn't necessarily the case – you may prefer to say 'the customer is nearly always right' or 'the customer is king'. But whichever you choose, your customers need to be satisfied in order to buy from you more than once.

What will satisfy your customers and how do you know? Delivering satisfaction is what the whole business should be doing.

5 **Customer requirements** – These run quite closely with satisfaction, but you'll need to decide what is reasonable (and by whose standards) in terms of customer requirements. Think about how you will manage expectations here. If you're delivering fast food and you say 'second to none' in your marketing materials, can you actually deliver faster than all the competition? If your customer requires a tailor-made version of each of your products and you can't do that, how will you respond?

6 **Profit** – Unless it's delivering a service profitably, your company will go out of business. The franchise model that you are working to must show where your profit is going to come from.

To make these six elements come to life, imagine you are going to set up a market fruit stall. All the questions below must be answered in your marketing strategy. Apply them to your business, whether franchisee or franchisor.

- At which market are you going to set up your stall?
- On which days will you run it?
- What products will you sell?

- How much will you charge for them?
- How will you let your customers know when you'll be at the market?
- How will you tell potential customers what you sell, where, when and at what price?
- How will you let people know where in the marketplace you are?
- How will you stop people buying from other stallholders instead of from you?
- How are you going to make sure they remember who you are so they can come back and buy from you again?
- How will you behave towards your customers to make them want to come back?
- What can you do to make sure they recommend you to all their friends?
- What will you do if anyone complains to make sure they don't stop buying from you?
- How are you going to minimise the risk of them complaining?
- How will you know if there are other products they would like to buy from you if only you stocked them?
- If you stock items too large for the customers to carry home, are you going to deliver them? How and at what price?

Market-led versus product-led. Which approach is going to ensure you have a viable business – market-led or product-led? Have a look at the examples below. The first is the only one that is market-led. Of course the idea will require some market research, but the principle is that if you are providing something people want or can be persuaded to need, you're on the right track.

1   There are lots of sporty, horse-riding and golfing people around here, so I reckon there are a good few fishing enthusiasts. But there's nowhere to fish. I wonder whether I could dig a lake in my field, turn it into a trout farm, and charge people for coarse fishing?

2   I'd like to be my own boss and I've never really used all those skills I picked up at art college. I really like painting on china – maybe I should sell hand-painted china mugs.

3   I've invented an ingenious attachment for a food mixer that grinds up the ends of soap bars and mixes them together into a fresh bar of soap. I could go into business selling it.

4   I've just noticed that the car roof-rack is constructed similarly to a sledge. I could make roof-racks that people can take off and turn into sledges for their kids in the winter.

5   I'd love to take the kids sledging but there isn't
    room on the car for a decent-sized sledge. What
    I need is one that attaches to the roof – then I
    could strap their bicycles and tennis rackets to it
    as well.

Get to know your customers!

Customers operate on two levels:

1   rational/ functional
2   irrational/emotional

Whatever they're buying, both levels will come into the
decision-making process. The following two questions need to
be explored if you are to truly know your customers:

1   **How do they feel about your product?** Does it make
    them feel good? Do they like what is says about
    them?
2   **What do they think about your product?** Do they
    understand it? Do they think its features and
    benefits are superior to those supplied by the
    competition and can meet their needs? Do they feel
    that your product is good value, given its benefits
    and costs?

Seven cornerstones of marketing

What really matters in marketing are the points of contact between the customer and your communications, products and people. These elements constitute your marketing, from a customer's point of view.

When does a customer interact with people, product or information? *Brainstorm using the seven Ps, below:*

1. Product – What aspects of the product itself are important or have an influence on customer purchase intentions? Think about tangibles and intangibles; needs; look and feel; packaging.

List the aspects (rational features and emotional impressions) of your product that influence customer perception.

2. Price – How much does it cost the customer to obtain and use your product? Think about discounts; disposal of old product; extra costs; special offers.

List aspects of price that influence customer perception.

3. Place – When and where can your customers buy your product?

List the aspects of place (in both time and space) that influence accessibility of your product.

4. Promotion – This incorporates any and every way in which you promote your product. As well as advertising, customer service and so on, think about invoices, admin, third-party behaviours (such as delivery people and so on) etc. that will affect your customers' perception of your product.

List all the ways you can promote your product offering to customers and prospects.

5. People – All points of human contact are important. People need to be trained and motivated to put across the right image for the marketing of a product.

List all the points of human contact that may be important to the success of marketing: sales, reception, service, accounts, repair, admin and premises.

6. Process – It's about more than just buying a product; what happens before and after?

- Are you identifying prospective customers effectively?
- How did they find you?
- What happens if the product breaks?

■ Do you have a delivery day process?

■ What's your complaints procedure?

List the processes involved in delivering the product and service.

7. Physical presence – Whether you're selling products or services, portraying the right image is important. Pay close attention to your premises (especially those that will be seen by customers), vehicles, appearance of staff and so on.

Strategy – the big picture

The core strategy of the business is the hub around which all marketing activities rotate. Look at the example on the following page, about the gift shop at an art gallery. The owner's strategic goal was to get gallery visitors to come into the shop and make a substantial purchase. Each tactic, developed by the staff, took them towards that goal.

Do a SWOT analysis of your current position

If you know where you are now, it gives a starting point to take you towards your goal – creating a marketing strategy. Generally speaking, a review of external factors will cover

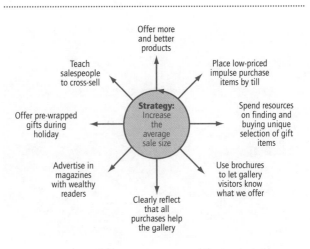

customers and competitors. Combined with an internal review about your own company, you have a SWOT analysis. Rather than focusing heavily on the negative aspects, or looking through rose-tinted spectacles at only the positive elements, think of a SWOT analysis as a balance sheet.

With a proper SWOT analysis you'll be in a better position to make strategic decisions that will be based on information and facts. This will in turn reduce the risk in decision-making.

Within the company		In the environment	
Strengths	+	Opportunities	+
Weaknesses	–	Threats	–

Within the company: you will focus on maintaining and enhancing strengths, whilst addressing weaknesses.

In the business environment: you will seek to exploit opportunities and minimise the impact of threats on your business.

Examples of SWOT factors are as follows:

Strengths include:
    special product
    high level service
    management awareness of the market
    national network
Weaknesses include:
    inadequate working capital
    poor management skills
    no experience in this market (this could also be an opportunity)
Opportunities include:
    gaps in the market
    changing tastes
    unsatisfied needs
Threats include:
    competitive action
    legislation (red tape)
    market trends

When you think of a threat as an opportunity in disguise, your approach may well change!

PESTLE

While a SWOT analysis looks at the day-to-day factors affecting your business, PESTLE is a management technique that is helpful in understanding the external environment in which an organisation operates, i.e. the outside influences on success or failure. This section is most relevant for a franchisor as you consider the long-term implications of your business in a global market.

The environment we live in can be wonderful, or it can be horrible, and sometimes it can be a mixture of both. Any form of organisation, whether it is a one-person business, a multinational company or a national utility, has its own **internal** strengths and weaknesses, but the world outside will also have a major **external** influence on success or failure.

- **P**olitical – the current and potential influences from political pressures. For example: taxation, privatisation, deregulation, international trade regulations, government stability, international stability
- **E**conomic – the local, national and world economy impact. For example: interest rates, money supply, credit control, inflation, financial markets, competitors' pricing, globalisation
- **S**ociological – the ways in which changes in society affect us. For example: mobility, income

distribution, population demographics, attitude to work and leisure, standards of education and skills, working conditions

- **Technological** – how new and emerging technology affects our business. For example: IT development, new materials and processes, government technology funding, software upgrades
- **Legal** – how local, national and world legislation affects us. For example: employment law, trade and product restrictions, health and safety regulations, EU and international laws, Monopolies Commission
- **Environmental** – the local, national and world environmental issues. For example: pollution problems, planning permissions, waste disposal, noise controls, environmental pressure groups

The problem with external factors is that they are continuously changing. When doing a PESTLE analysis, it's important to look at what's affecting the business *now* and what could affect it in the future.

The six PESTLE factors may be applied to the whole of the organisation, or to specific business areas, or to specific parts of business areas, in order to consider the likely implications.

Business areas could include:

- customers
- franchisees
- technology
- the industry/marketplace
- intermediaries
- competitors
- other stakeholders

Following a PESTLE analysis, and in order to take decisions, the internal strengths and weaknesses of the business must be assessed. These areas could include:

- the resources (assets)
- the size and structure
- the culture and style
- the relationship with employees
- the relationship with franchisees
- the corporate image
- the skills
- the track record
- the rewards
- leadership

Sales promotion and advertising methods

The elements that come under the banner of marketing are, generally speaking, as follows:

- advertising
- public and customer relations
- website (see 'Internet' section below)
- networking

Advertising

Wouldn't it be lovely if you could just advertise your product and wait for the orders to roll in! If only business was that simple. However, the purpose of a promotional strategy is to move a potential buyer from having never heard of you to buying your product. The process looks like this:

Unawareness
Awareness
Comprehension
Conviction
Action

Obviously, the object is to take your specific target audience through these steps. With the correct message, media selection and evaluation, you will learn what works. It's a numbers game, so be sure to think about how you will evaluate success. Revenue? Number of new customers? Average spend? Increased spend?

The first thing to think about is how you are going to reach your audience. You simply cannot afford to reach millions of people who will never buy your product, so you need to choose your advertising methods carefully. Here are some of the choices:

National newspapers – Large, general audience, can be defined at a socio-economic level, e.g. *The Times* versus *The Sun*. However, newspaper advertising is expensive and it's difficult to stand out from the crowd. In addition, newspaper audience levels are reducing with the increase in online and other alternative media formats such as mobile phones.

Regional newspapers – Smaller, more specific audiences at this geographical level.

Television – Large audience, but with satellite TV they are now fragmented and harder and more expensive to reach.

Posters – A variety of formats locally and nationally. Need succinct message. Can be really cost-efficient when well planned and executed.

Radio (local) – Definable market, i.e. 'travel to work' and general 'at home' audience. Works well with posters.

Cinema – Strong, national brands can use this effectively. Local advertisers can buy packages but beware cheap ads, locally produced, that don't reflect your image well.

Direct mail – Can be targeted specifically so you can reach a specified group. Has it been done to death? Only go down this route if you are working with an experienced business with a solid, proven track record.

Internet – Thousands of opportunities here. Beware of sharks.

Don't forget that everything seen by the customer or potential customer is advertising who you are and what you do. Brochures, letters, invoices, customer service, vans, offices, even the loos, send a message about your business.

What message are you delivering?

- Buy one, get one free
- Sale starts today
- Sale ends Friday
- New Series 10, out now
- Free massage with every bar of soap
- We've done our own ads and they look cheap/nasty!

When spending money on advertising ask the following questions:

- What is the specific goal of this ad?
- What will my customers think of it?
- How will I know if it's worked?
- What's the competition up to?
- When is the best time to advertise?
- Who can help me to make this a success?
- Is this just about my ego?

PR

PR rarely sells products directly, but it's still more than worthwhile. PR will assist you in promoting a strong, positive image for your business. As a result:

- People are more likely to buy your product or service if they like your company.
- People will be more likely to recommend you to others.
- Your name and product are more likely to be remembered.
- You will find it easier to attract and retain good staff.
- Suppliers will be more keen to get your business.

It's true that you can manage without PR, but with it you will become more effective. Handled well, PR can head off bad press at the pass and help to keep you in front of the competition. If you handle your PR internally it's virtually free, which must be good news!

There are likely to be two kinds of image that you want to publicise:

1   A general, feel-good impression of the
    business – friendly, successful, good to work
    for etc.
2   Specific aspects of the business that are key image
    points – efficient, smart, and so on.

Generally speaking there are three ways in which to get this image across using PR:

1   In the papers
2   On the radio/television
3   Other routes (charity events, sponsorship etc.)

Networking

Networking comes into the face-to-face selling as well as PR and communications categories. There will always be a thousand opportunities for you to network at breakfasts, lunches and dinners. Be sure that the organisers want to make money as well as giving you the opportunity to enter into new business relationships. Making the most of your business contacts at networking events makes sense but can also generate disproportionate levels of stress.

A good return on investment is important for all your marketing activity. Keep a close track of what you spend and how effective each activity is in generating revenue/profit. Networking lunches may be great fun, but does the £3000 you spend a year on them generate you any business?

Marketing jargon buster

You'll hear all sorts of marketing-speak that can seem daunting if this is a new area for you. Below is a short jargon-buster that will clarify some of the terminology. If you are being baffled by jargon at any point, don't assume you should know – ask!

AIDA	Attention, Interest, Desire, Action
Above the line	advertising in press, TV or other media
Below the line	promotions that are not direct advertisements, such as reduced price offers and premiums
Brainstorm	two heads are better than one. When ideas are scarce or you

	need to resolve a problem, get together for a brainstorm
Brands	the distinguishing proprietary name, symbol or trademark that differentiates a particular product or service from others of a similar nature
Brief	the outline of what needs to be done on any project
Copy	what you call an article when it's being written and before publication
Demographics	statistics that tell you about society and consumers, e.g. births, deaths and age profiles of populations
Direct marketing	getting the information to individuals, usually done by post, telephone, e-mail or text
Distribution	the selection of distribution channels, i.e. ways of making the product available to the target audience
FMCG	fast-moving consumer goods, i.e.

	products we eat or use quickly, such as food and drink
Market position	(or market share). Mine's bigger than yours! Finding out who's getting most business in a market by comparing your productivity and success with your competitors
Market segment	segmentation divides the market into distinct subsets (segments) that behave in a similar way or have similar needs. Some variables could be geographic, demographic, psychographic or behavioural.
Positioning	shows where you stand in the market
PR	public relations – generating positive publicity about products or organisations
Press release	a statement issued by an organisation and sent to the press – anything from news on a product

	launch to a comment on a business scandal
Promotions	involve informing and persuading customers to buy
Strap lines	the slogan or catchphrase that appears on an advert, e.g. 'Men can't help acting on Impulse'
Targeting	choosing which segments you are going to address
The total market	the total amount spent on the satisfaction of a need, irrespective of the products which satisfy the need
Unique selling point (USP)	a product's single attribute that makes it a saleable commodity and enables it to stand out against its competitors

As a franchisor, you must have a clear marketing strategy that can be easily picked up, understood and adhered to by your franchisees. Your brand integrity is at stake if you allow maverick-style marketing at a local level. You would be as well to have templates for franchisees to use freely, making clear the elements that are interchangeable. For financial and legal areas of your franchise business you must use an expert in that area. Marketing is no exception – spend wisely!

Key points

■ Keep your marketing effort simple.
■ Understand what flexibility you have for marketing within your franchise agreement.
■ As a franchisor, you must protect your brand fiercely. Don't allow it to be undermined in any way by anyone. Use your franchise agreement wisely in this area.

Things to watch out for

■ Baffling jargon.
■ Spending too much money on marketing without any return on investment.
■ Good marketing courses that you can attend.

Helpful resources

■ Chartered Institute of Marketing – **www.cim.co.uk**
■ *Boosting Sales on a Shoestring* by Bob Gorton
ISBN 978-0-7136-7541-2
■ *Steps to Success: Network with confidence*
ISBN 978-0-7136-8146-8

INDEX